The
DANCE
of
TIME

The
DANCE
of
TIME

The Origins of the Calendar:

*A Miscellany of
History and Myth,
Religion and Astronomy,
Festivals and
Feast Days*

MICHAEL JUDGE

Arcade Publishing • New York

FIRST EDITION

Library of Congress Cataloging-in-Publication Data
Judge, Michael.
  The dance of time : the origins of the calendar : a miscellany of history and myth, religion and astronomy, festivals and feast days / by Michael Judge. —1st ed.
    p. cm.
  ISBN 1-55970-746-1
  1. Calendar—History. I. Title.

  CE6.J83 2004
  529'.3 — dc22   2004009480

Published in the United States by Arcade Publishing, Inc.,
New York
Distributed by Time Warner Book Group

Visit our Web site at www.arcadepub.com

10 9 8 7 6 5 4 3 2 1

Designed by API

EB

PRINTED IN THE UNITED STATES OF AMERICA

For Nancy and Phyllis

The river runs, the round world spins
Dawn and lamplight, midnight, noon.
Sun follows day, night stars and moon.
The day ends, the end begins.

—Jean Renoir

Contents

PART ONE

The Tale of Years

CHAPTER ONE

And Life Time's Fool

Starting now the hours of the clock
Will hang on a hair around my neck
Starting now the stars will stop
In their courses sun cock-crow shadows
And everything that time proclaimed
Is now deaf and dumb and blind
For me all nature is silenced
With the ticking of the law and its measure.

— Friedrich Nietzsche

 he flowing river of time, carrying us from inception to eternity, is both invention and illusion; a phantom child of mortal dreams and fears. So the scientists tell us. They assure us that velocity can stretch time like wool spun on a distaff, and that relativity makes time merely another variable in a host of equations whirling around the universe.

Certainly our time, Western time, the spliced and segregated seconds, minutes, and hours by which we regulate our busy lives, was an invention of the late Middle Ages. Before then, time was measured naturally, and by those things of which it was made: the sun, the moon, and the stars; revolving watches of sleepy soldiers; human criers at dawn and cattle lowing in the gloaming; burning tapers during peace and burning cities during war; national disasters and signal triumphs; the reigns of kings, the death of princes, the fall of empires; comets and their strikes, freakish births, sudden miracles, and the rumor of dragons; heavy rains, sweeping plagues, hard winters, and sudden springs; and, of course, by church bells tolling, cocks crowing, and sand bleeding through the hourglass.

In ancient days, the world itself served as a vast clock. People closely watched the seasons change: winter thawed into spring, which warmed into summer; summer surrendered to cool autumn, until the first freeze of winter descended and the cycle began again.

The heavens kept time with the earth. The sun dependably marked off the day's hours as it journeyed westward across the sky: one circuit of the sun from dawn to dawn is, in fact, the very definition of a day. The sun also acted like any sensible person, retreating from winter's cold and returning with the warming days of spring.

After sunset, in any season, the lambent moon rose to guide travelers through the night. The moon also, mysteriously but conveniently, changed its shape, growing from thin crescent to full orb and shrinking back to crescent again in a cycle that took about twenty-nine days. The inconstant moon proved a reliable measure for longer stretches of time, from new moon to new moon. The ancient Germans called this period of about thirty days a *monath*; and, but for a sliding vowel, so do we still.

From the most ancient times, people recognized that the earthly and celestial turning points of the year were linked. The sun's travels delineated the seasons. The solstices, when the sun reached its farthest northern and southern position in the sky, inaugurated summer and winter; the equinoxes, when the sun stood midway between the solstices and the length of day and night were equal, marked the advent of spring and autumn.

The gauzy night sky held other signposts. Certain stars appeared annually, like heralds announcing the seasons. Throughout the Western world, the great hourglass-shaped constellation of Orion warned of impending winter, while Leo the lion's right triangle marked a sure sign of spring. The Pleiades, so diaphanously lovely that to really see them one had to look the other way, led summer into fall.

All nature obeyed the dictates of cyclical time, not least human beings. Just as the sun waned from blazing summer strength to a feeble spark on the far horizon, so too did the young eventually grow old; just as the trees in the forests and the crops in the fields withered with the onset of fall, so too did human beings age, sicken, and die. Nature yearly reiterated the life cycle of humankind, and each individual's fate reflected the dance of the cosmos.

These cycles of time, and the mysterious connection between people and their surrounding universe, were codified in sacred festivals, temporal maps charting out the course of the year as mariners charted voyages. The great festivals of the year, held at the solstices, equinoxes, and important agricultural turning points, ritualized this connection between the cycles of human life and those of the natural world.

Festivals marked out the progress of the year. They celebrated the return of the sun after the winter solstice, marked spring's first planting under favorable stars, called revelers to delight in the flowering May, and solemnly observed the final whispering night of autumn. They also loaned the power of ritual to life's simple necessities: ripening crops, the birth of new flocks, ice breaking on a river, the day the rains came. These simple events took on a patina of sanctity, of destiny, in a world still ruled by neighborhood gods.

Although life was shorter, time was longer, moving with the steady but unhurried sun from one season to the next, changing in increments with the moon, wheeling with the great circle of the stars.

Then, around 1350, carefully stowed beneath the decks of trading ships, keeping company with gunpowder

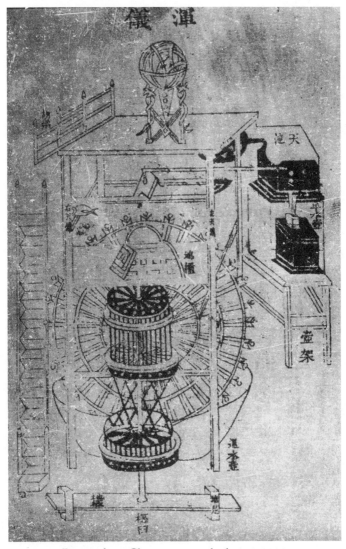

Design for a Chinese water clock, A.D. 1008.

and the astrolabe, the first mechanical clocks arrived in Europe. Modern time made its debut, and changed its creators.

Modeled on the ancient Chinese water tower, early clocks used falling drops of water to count out the seconds and minutes of the day. For fourteenth-century observers, accustomed to marking the hours by the shouts of town criers and the tolling of church bells, the first clocks must have been startling reminders of humanity's bondage to time, counting out the seconds as misers counted coins. Moreover, with an ear bent toward the new machine, one could literally hear time fall; one drop of water after the other stealing the seconds away.

Shakespeare may have caught something of this anxious mood and placed it in the dying mouth of the gallant rebel Hotspur in *Henry IV, Part 1*. A man of great humor and courage, Hotspur nonetheless is representative of the old medieval order, the old way of seeing things. Like a knight charging a cannon, he flies to his death at the hands of Prince Hal, who will go on to decimate many medieval notions on the plains of Agincourt.

"Oh Thought's the slave of life," Hotspur gasps in Hal's arms, "and life time's fool." Hotspur, the child of a slow-moving, expansive, and natural world, makes the final realization that time, like his thoroughly modern enemy Henry V, is a force to be reckoned with.

Although rare and expensive, early clocks were woefully inaccurate by modern standards, losing as much as half an hour a day. The invention of the verge-and-foliot mechanism, in which a wooden escarpment seized a turning gear at exact intervals to count out seconds, made clocks more precise. That crucial gear connected to more shafts, spinning still more gears, connected to even more shafts. So clocks remained large, unwieldy devices: networks of brass gears, wooden phalanges, iron pendulums, and leather pulleys, encased in finely wrought cabinets that dominated the hallways of the rich and royal.

In 1502 Peter Heinlein, an enterprising German clock maker, produced the Nuremberg Egg, the world's first portable clock. What once stood in palaces could now rest on a merchant's mantel. Some years later, the invention of the self-winding spring ensured that a clock could carry its own coiled power source. The watch had arrived, and time itself could be carried.

Gradually, it began to carry its carriers. No longer an aspect of divinity, time became a commodity: it could be bought, sold, bartered for, wasted. In the seventeenth century, Sir Isaac Newton recast the universe as an enormous, precise, and incontrovertible clock, with planets and stars whirling out their unchanging paths through infinite reaches of space and time. Once upon a time, people had named the stars by which they measured their passage through the year, and created constellations that recalled heroes and goddesses, instruments, and animals: whole mythologies painted in starlight from horizon to horizon. After Newton, people no longer seemed a part of the night sky's now remote procession.

The old festivals, which had sanctified humanity's connection to the universe, gradually lost their sacred meaning and, though still observed, became secular occasions: revels held in honor of connections long severed, rituals long forgotten, gods long dead. Time gradually stopped being a reflection of the natural world, and became a mechanism.

Now nature itself has been mechanized in the service of time, one second being measured, by international agreement, as the precise interval it takes for an atom of the element cesium to make 9,192,631,770 vibrations, spilling its coiled energy into the cooling universe, hastening the frantic world on, marking time.

All the while, the old world watches. Embedded in our technological age, there remains an ancient artifact, a reminder of the days before mechanical time, when the rhythms of earth and sky matched those of man and woman. This strange survivor still recalls an ancient way of seeing, still celebrates the seasons and their different moods: the sun in his azure sky, the eerie moon wrapped in her mantle of stars, and the habits, sacred and profane, of mortal beings. It has, over many centuries, woven the festivals, observances, and customs of humanity into a tapestry on which the lineaments of human life may still be traced. It is called the calendar.

Unlike a watch or a clock, the calendar does not presume to duplicate time. Instead, it serves as a landscape of time, a description not of the thing itself, but of what the thing may mean; a cry not for scientific precision but for emotional understanding. Unlike other timekeeping devices, the calendar is organic: a social contract reminding hurried modern creatures of their debt to nature and to the past.

Most people have forgotten, having surrendered their time to mechanisms, why Halloween falls at the end of October, why the birth of Christ is proclaimed in winter's darkness, why Easter and Passover come hand in hand with the spring. Yet it is exactly in answering these questions that we discover a remarkable world, far and yet near, ancient and yet as new as tomorrow's sunrise, where symbol and reality conjoin.

I mean this: in late autumn, with the shadows growing, the calendar summons children to carve leering faces into pumpkin flesh; a tribute, though they do not know it, to all of their dead ancestors, returning for one night from the loam, and a reminder, though they need not yet heed it, of the ghosts that they will one day become.

The calendar fences the latter days of December away from the rest of the common year, commanding the vulgar world to pause and await the birth of the savior and his symbol, the returning sun.

The calendar commands that Easter can only occur after the vernal equinox, when Christ returns amid robins and blooming hyacinth, lengthening days, and sudden rains, and, like nature after winter's cruelty, is reconciled to the world.

Halloween and the death of the year, Christmas lights shining in the depths of winter, Easter services held at the rising of the gentle spring sun: these things, the simplest things, recall a universe in which we were not strangers. That universe is with us still — in fact it lies one step beyond the stoop. Its story is ours, as old as humanity. Its cast is immense — wind and weather, stars and saints, kings and peasants — and the lead is none other than dear old Mother Earth herself, who waltzes around our sun in stately time, trailing the seasons in her train. Yet for many, that world remains hidden, just out of sense, like the half-heard murmur of an underground stream. Uncovering that stream, and inviting you to drink from its waters, is the purpose of this book.

CHAPTER TWO

The Marriage of Heaven and Earth

All praise be yours, my Lord, for all that you have made.
First, my brother Sun, who brings the day
And shines your light upon us.
How beautiful he is, how radiant in splendor;
Of you he bears the likeness.

Praise be to you, dear Lord, for sister moon and stars,
So beautiful and radiant and clear

— Saint Francis of Assisi, "The Canticle of the Sun"

odern scientists and their ancient forerunners share a common perception across the gulf of years: that the world and time are one. The motion of the first creates the latter; the grinding of the second wears away the first. Ancient philosophers and astrologers knew little of what we call physics, but they knew that the world of their mortal labors and the larger, natural world were intimately connected. They chose to explain this connection through a combination of rough science and precise poetry, ascribing to gods and goddesses the changing seasons, weather patterns, the lives and wanderings of animals, the flowering and fading of plants, and — most profoundly, because most removed from the quotidian — the journeys of the planets and the motion of the stars.

The ancients found changes in the earthly world rather easy to explain. Animals and plants were close at hand, and resembled men and women in their lives and responses to the seasons. Animals ate, coupled and reared young, fled from the cold of winter and basked in summer's warmth. Plants grew like children, drank water, and thrived or withered with the wheeling of the year. Beasts could be herded, and plants could be gathered. The world of the earth surrounded mankind, available for inspection and manipulation.

The sky offered no such partnership. The vital sun, the wandering moon, the star-daubed path of the Milky Way: these sights presented unfathomable mysteries. The true nature of the lights above seemed utterly unknowable, a secret treasure of the gods. For thousands of years people thought it best simply to watch and to worship. The sky, overarching, endless, redolent of eternity, was humanity's first cathedral.

*   *   *

The first people who made the sky a subject of recorded analysis settled in the Tigris-Euphrates river valley (now Iraq) about seven thousand years ago. We know them as the Sumerians, and they were industrious folk. On the low plains of Mesopotamia, the Sumerians developed the fundamental elements of civilization: writing, cities, a sophisticated political system, organized religion, and beer.

The Sumerian view of the cosmos came from what they saw around them: a looming sky, and a dense, stygian mystery beneath the feet. Ki, the flat disk of the earth, and An, the overarching bowl of heaven (made of precious tin), were born from Abzu, the primordial sea. Shining within An's wide vault lay Lil, the atmosphere; its gases had long ago congealed to form the sun, the moon, the planets, and the stars. Up there, amid the shimmering lights, dwelt the gods. Deep below the earth lay a dark and gloomy underworld, lair of blood-drinking ghosts and pestilent demons, whose thick cries could be heard during earthquakes. Evil seemed to come from below; the good must surely lie above, in the lights.

Casting their patient eyes and probing minds toward the lights of heaven, the Sumerians slowly learned to measure the passage of heavenly bodies over the earth.

They marked the important turning points of the sun's journey, the solstices and equinoxes. They followed the moon and stars with equal fervor, and unlike the sky watchers of earlier, illiterate eras, they wrote down what they saw.

The Sumerians became the first human beings to record for succeeding generations, for us, the astonishing fact that the essential events of their lives — the growth of crops, the rising and falling of rivers, the mating and birth of animals, and all the other marvels of the world —

The Sumerian sun god Shamash receiving homage from three small figures.

seemed to be in thrall to the wanderings of the sun, the moon, and the stars.

They learned that the celestial events corresponding with the earthly could be used as markers reminding people when to go about the various tasks involved in earning a living. When a certain star that had not been seen for many months rose just after twilight, it was time to sow. Another star called in the harvest. And they began to recognize and record whole groups of stars, tracing the outlines of deities or fabulous animals between the distant points of light: the constellations.[1]

Religion and astronomy were inseparable, just as the dictates of astronomer-priests presented farmers and herdsmen with a reliable almanac of the working year. Astronomy began not as science, as we understand it, but as an attempt to capture the elusive designs of the gods.

Gods whom the Sumerians worshipped, but did not trust. Gloomy, apt Sumerian poetry still warns man that his life is a bitter, mocking gift; that he is dust in the great wind of the ages, and that all of his works last but a little moment. So it proved with the grandparents of

---

[1]You may think them foolish, but when I was very young, my father taught me quite a few of the constellations by bundling me up and taking me out into the backyard on cold November nights and making his arm a pointer along which I could gaze. He showed me the belt of Orion, then the hourglass of Orion's outstretched arms and feet. After a moment, I saw a man walking in the sky. I still do.

Western culture. The Sumerians, so busy at so many graceful, unwarlike things, had a pathetic idea of an army and were defeated and defeated again: by Akkadians and Hittites, Assyrians and Persians. As a power, they passed away; as a people, they infected their conquerors with the subtlety of their thought, and taught them to observe and measure the wandering lights of An. As a power they passed away; but in all the subsequent empires founded on their fall, Sumerian astronomy became the thing to do — the hobby of kings and the duty of priests — and Sumerian mathematics, the standard of education. After all, the good of the state depended on correctly mapping the lights through which divinity silently spoke. The Sumerians made astronomy. Their conquerors made it stick.

In another part of the Levant, a small nation of nomadic herdsmen developed a theology that was destined to abolish the pantheons of earlier religions. These remarkable people were the Hebrews, who some six thousand years ago came to the simple conclusion that the world — the universe — was in the care of one god, and one god only. They would suffer for this belief, at the hands of many empires; but the faith they had in the single and unnameable father of the cosmos burned like a sacred tabernacle throughout their history, as it does to this day. This remarkable declaration made the relationship between humanity and its creator not so much a trial as a blood relationship: not so much a forced call to placation as an invitation to worship and to prayer.

Not all early astronomers were driven to look up for purely practical reasons. Immortality flickered in the stars that, night after night, appeared only a stone's throw above the twilight. A longing having nothing to do with prediction must have seized anybody who beheld the countless lights that burned, in those eras before electric light and industrial haze, with a glory we can only imagine. The ancients raised their ziggurats and pyramids so that they could literally climb closer to heaven, gazing from the earthly home of men and women into the starry pasturelands of the creators; an act not only of science, nor even of dutiful religion, but of awe, delight, and love. An anonymous Babylonian poet who lived around 1500 B.C. calls forth the constellations like Prospero his elves:

> Heaven, the father of the poor,
> The judge has gone into his chamber.
> May the gods of the night come forth:
>
> Irra, the valiant; the Goat; the Bison;
> Girra the shining; the seven; the Dragon—
> May the stars come forth in the high heaven!

Of course none of these ancient stargazers knew that we live on a planet circling a medium-sized, middle-aged star at the outer edge of a spiral galaxy. Trusting their eyes and common sense, they naturally assumed themselves to be at the heart of things: on a flat (possibly round, but that was an issue for philosophers) earth in the center of a spherical universe. This vision of the world held true from distant China to the gray Atlantic, from the most sophisticated Chaldean astrologers clambering up the sandstone steps of the great ziggurat in Babylon to the shaggiest Celtic druids notching the phases of the moon on oak staffs in the gloom-haunted forests of Hibernia.

The universe of old was also very small by modern standards of measurement. Even the Greeks, whose questions about the world around them initiated the first genuine attempts at science, assumed that the sun was about the size of a shield. The moon was no larger than a chariot, and the stars were literally heaven's lamps: shining pinpoints of light strung like diadems through the raven tresses of night. They imagined earth as a disk nestled between the Olympian realm high above and the sere land of Hades, underworld of whispering shades, below. To explain how this tidy, poetic universe had come about, Greek bards sang stories of the gods, stories so beautiful that they continue to illuminate the Western imagination.

Long ago, claims the Greek creation myth, Uranus the sky wed Gaia the earth. Their lovemaking produced the oceans and the lands, the trees, the flowers and animals. The marriage of heaven and earth finally produced men and women, who saw in the connection between the cycles of the sky and the cycles of the earth proof that they and their world were together children of the gods.

Alexander the Great, in spite of being tutored by the pragmatist Aristotle, believed in the tales of Uranus and Gaia and all of their Olympian offspring and undoubtedly clung to notions of the universe common in the Greece of his day: a small world sitting under a low-slung sky, like a table beneath a campaigner's tent.

Early in his life, before he embarked on his extraordinary campaigns, Alexander feasted a wandering band of Celts near the mouth of the Danube. Impressed by the Celts' insistence that, if invaded, they would fight and die, singing, to the last man, Alexander asked if there was anything they were afraid of. Of course, one of the warriors assured him. He and his friends often trembled to think that the sky might fall on their heads.

Alexander threw back his golden head and laughed; but their low and perilous sky was also his.

Alexander chose the sun god Apollo as his divine champion and model. It is not surprising that he did so. The sun dominated the daytime sky and moved with dependable regularity across it. It appeared every morning at dawn, no matter what calamities had dropped on the globe in the dark. From recognition of this common miracle came the most basic unit of the calendar, the day.

Days were probably first measured from dawn to dawn, a period lasting roughly twenty-four hours — the time it takes for the earth to make one full rotation in space.

To the ancients, however, the sun, not the earth, did the moving, rising in glory at dawn and coursing slowly through the sky until it set below the western horizon.

The Greeks worshipped the sun as the demigod Helios, and imagined him a shining charioteer drawn by a team of golden horses through the sky. They tendered a lovely explanation for what became of him during the dark hours of night. After traversing the heavens, Helios returned to his golden palace in the far west, where he watered his weary horses and bathed himself in the cool ocean to renew his power. Even gods must sleep, and Helios would recline on his golden chariot to doze while being drawn eastward through the bowels of the earth by attending nymphs. When he woke, he vaulted once more into the sky at the heels of his rosy herald Eos, the dawn.

The sun not only marked off the days; it also measured out the larger year. Observers couldn't help but notice that, for all of its seeming regularity, the sun strayed north and south through the seasons. While it blazed away almost directly overhead in summer, bathing the earth in light fiery enough to redden the skin, after the summer solstice, which literally means "sun stop," the sun paused in its northward path and slowly began retreating south. The days shortened and the air cooled; winter settled on the land. By midwinter, the sun was a spark flickering at the southern horizon.

At this very moment, as if by magic, the sun stopped fleeing and slowly came north again. With it came the spring, followed by the summer, until the sun would halt its tracks and the cycle began again. This cycle, 365 days from any one point to any other, is the year; one full circle of our planet's perpetual journey around her star.

The people who observed the frightful retreat and joyful return of the sun did not know that its cause is nothing more than a slight tilt of the earth, which orbits the sun at an angle of 23.4 degrees. When the northern hemisphere is inclined toward the sun, it receives a greater share of light, and long summer days commence. The summer solstice, which falls on or about June 21, marks the greatest extent of this tilt toward the sun. When the north is tilted away from the sun's light and warmth, winter falls; the winter solstice, falling on or about December 21, marks the point at which the earth's angle is farthest away from the sun. Between these extremes, earth reaches two points in her orbit when she is entirely and evenly exposed to her native star. These are the equinoxes, when night and day last equally long, and they mark the advent of spring and fall.[2]

The sun, then, followed a rising and falling path through the sky during the course of the year. Greek astronomers named this invisible path the ecliptic: literally, the place where eclipses happen. The planets, of which the ancients knew seven, also traveled along this track — a result of the fact that the planets in our solar system all lie roughly in the same plane. The ecliptic was naturally thought of as a celestial highway, used by the sun and the planets to travel through the heavens.

Long before such things were recorded, people probably kept close track of the ecliptic, and carefully noted the moments of solstice and equinox: the first calendars, notched into stone or bark, recorded these moments of transition and allowed Stone Age commu-

---

[2]This can be hard to grasp, but here's a trick. Make a fist and point your knuckles toward a lamp. Imagine that your fist is the earth, and your knuckles the Northern Hemisphere. Pointed toward the lamp, your knuckles are illuminated. Rotate your hand. The knuckles remain in light. It's summertime. Now move your hand to the other side of the lamp, but keep the angle of your fist constant. Your knuckles should now point away from the light, and be in shadow. It's winter. Rotate your hand. The knuckles remain in shadow; the back of your hand enjoys the light. To see the equinoxes, just put your fist on either side of the lamp, keeping your angle constant. Rotate your hand. With every turn of the wrist, whichever side of your hand faces that tiny GE sun will be evenly bathed in light.

nities to tally the months and years. Later, hunting and farming schedules and the correct timing of religious rites depended on an even more accurate log of the sun. Calendars became more complex, and temples became observatories, early computers by which the motion of the seasonal sun was recorded, measured, and predicted. The most famous surviving of these remarkable structures is the Neolithic temple of Stonehenge in Salisbury, England, which predates classical Greek civilization by some 2,700 years and still invites the sun to rise over its hele stone on Midsummer Day.

About twenty miles north of Stonehenge, far less known but imbued with even more power, sits the immense megalithic temple of Avebury. Encompassing some thirty acres, it is the largest surviving henge in the world. A long esplanade of sarcen stones leads to two enormous concentric stone rings that encircle the modern town of Avebury, a typical Salisbury village, its tidy homes and cheerful pub set in the midst of a wonder. Why Avebury was constructed is still anybody's guess: some think that it was a place of sacrifice; others, that it represented the marriage of the earth goddess to the sky god, with the esplanade penetrating the circle in a phallic gesture of fertility. The most likely explanation is that Avebury, like Stonehenge, was meant to record the seasonal passage of the sun through the sky.

To stand in the midst of the immense circle of Avebury on a blustery English morning with wind hissing between the brooding pillars of sandstone is to feel something of the awe with which the ancient mind contemplated the universe. At least part of the builders' intention in raising this temple was to replicate the life and travels of their father, the sun, who would descend into this holy ring once a year to marry their mother, the earth. And their daughters' daughters' daughters somehow remember. Every year, on May Day, when the sun is still climbing toward glory and the earth has ripened beneath his strong but gentle hand, young women, who sense more of such things than their fathers will ever know, come to Avebury and sit among the stones.

The moon became another of humanity's celestial timekeepers. Unlike the sun — and with little rhyme or reason — the moon changed its shape, growing, as if with child, from a thin crescent to a full orb in about fifteen days. After two nights at the full, the moon dwindled, shrinking back to crescent, and finally vanished wholly into the dark of night. The complete cycle took twenty-nine days; a convenient, appropriately mysterious package of time that became used throughout the ancient world to track bundles of time longer than a day but shorter than a year.

Because the waxing and waning of the moon so closely resembled human pregnancy, and because its period matched that of a woman's menstrual cycle, the moon was worshipped as a goddess throughout the ancient world. Her various names reflect the lonely, silver beauty with which she bathes our dreams: Selene, Diana, Artemis. Representing the feminine to the sun's masculine power, she commanded the tender passions and powers of the night: sexuality, darkness, and magic.

Diana, Roman goddess of fertility.

The moon's light made lovers embrace all the tighter, and she oversaw all the secretive doings of the night. But as the dark mistress, she had a dangerous, unfathomable temperament and could at a whim slay her lovers or drive men mad: our word *lunacy* comes from the Latin word *luna*, the moon. The full moon was most perilous; belief is still widespread that the moon at her full induces violence, compulsions, and sexual abandon in mortals, as Shakespeare noted in *Othello*:

> Tis the very error of the moon;
> she comes more close to earth
> than was her wont, and drives men mad.

The founding Semitic civilizations of the Fertile Crescent — Sumerian, Babylonian, Israelite, Hittite, Egyptian, and many more — and later the Greeks and Romans, those children of the lapping sea between the lands who honed the guesses of their cultural fathers into disciplines called philosophy, poetry, drama, logic, and mathematics; they all of them based their sacred calendars on the cycles of the moon, and even reckoned their days from sunset to sunset. Ceremonies, festivals, important dates, and public rites were conducted according to her changes. If the sun measured out working time, the moon became the mistress of ritual time.

The stars and planets also helped people chart their way through the temporal sea of the year. The myriad stars revolved like a great pinwheel across the sky, anchored to a single celestial point — Polaris, the North Star, which in northern latitudes never sets. Most other stars, however, do rise and set with the seasons, and the ancients learned to use them very effectively as a luminous calendar.

From earliest days, sky watchers recognized a set of twelve groups of constellations that kept company with the sun and planets. These constellations always traveled within an area extending a little above and below the ecliptic. In the fifth century B.C., Babylonian sky watchers divided the ecliptic into twelve segments, each marked by one of these constellations. Most of them were named after real or fantastical animals; hence the term *zodiac*, which comes from a Greek word meaning "circle of animals."

The twelve constellations of the zodiac came to represent twelve distinct periods of the year, each of which began when the sun entered that particular constellation in its annual march. These constellations were not seen in the sky at these times; they literally rose with the sun, and so were invisible. Still, the skill of the ancient astronomers became so great that they could pinpoint the exact moment when a zodiacal constellation rose. These zodiacal signs were used by ancient astronomers to keep a complex, occult calendar of the year; they believed, as many still do, that each sign of the zodiac influenced human beings in a specific way.

*　　*　　*

Gradually, all of these observations became part of oral tradition. The Greek poet Hesiod (c. 700 B.C.) was the first to write down centuries of accumulated lore about the year. Although his reputation for surliness and misogyny is well deserved, Hesiod's description of the Greek year makes us privy to an ancient conversation, in which Mother Earth and Father Heaven still speak to their mortal children:

In the early fall, the Pleiades, a cluster of seven stars that shine like gauzy jewels above the horns of Taurus the bull, rise in the west. Their advent signals farmers to begin their plowing, lest they should sow the next year's crop too late. Earth offers other signs of autumn: the flight of migrating cranes, fluttering leaves, and sudden downpours warn the farmer that winter lurks over the next hill.

It soon comes, carried on the wide back of Orion the hunter, who rises with the first frosts. By the time of the winter solstice, cattle and goats should be safe in their snug pens, there to stay through deep winter. As long as Orion rules the gelid heavens, men and beasts alike should stay safely within smoky lodges and well-tended stables.

In early spring, the benevolent constellation of Boötes, the herdsman, with the red star Arcturus blazing at his heel, rises just after sunset. The celestial shepherd

Orion.

reminds his fellows below that the cattle should be released from their winter rest and put to the plow.

In April, the Pleiades dip below the horizon for forty days. When they rise again, summer follows at their lovely heels. In the woodlands, the cuckoo returns, and the immortal swallow; together they sing a bright paean to warming nights, inviting roaming lovers. Nature awakes and unfolds beneath the paws of Leo the lion, whose roar melts the final snows of winter and heartens the warming sun.

In midsummer the Zephyr, a gentle wind from the

west, tousles the hair and lessens the midday heat. Soon, however, Orion appears in the southern sky just before dawn: summer has reached its zenith. By July's end, Sirius, the Dog Star, rises with the sun. Although unseen, it invisibly dominates the sky, and the days grow hot and close. Now is the time for grape pressing, woodcutting, and gathering the first fruits of the season's harvest.

Harvest brings the wheel around. Soon enough the swallows that had sung spring's liberation will again be on the wing; soon enough the Pleiades will rise in beauty; soon enough the cranes, bound for Africa, will lift off on their great ebony wings, and the autumn rains will begin again. Soon enough the leaves will fall to die, and nourish through the winter the buried tubers waiting for another spring.

Shortly after his meeting with the Celts, Alexander stood on the banks of the Danube and gazed north. Stirred by Celtic tales of mysteries undreamed of beyond the horizon, he felt a stinging longing to follow the wide and willowed river off into the misty unknown. But Alexander had business elsewhere, and with a sigh of regret he turned toward Persia and the East.

At about the same time, a small city-state in Italy was consolidating its power over the peninsula. One hundred years after Alexander's meteoric rise and sudden death, Rome would dominate the Mediterranean; one hundred years later, it would control most of the Western world.

Roman legions would march in bronzed and leathered ranks deep into the lands of Alexander's youthful vision, bringing classical civilization north of the Alps, making Celts and Germans, Britains and Goths, citizens of the Eternal City. Among the many gifts that stern Rome gave its charges was a calendar that, but for a few changes, still measures the year. With customary bluntness, the Romans now demand their hour.

CHAPTER THREE

Calendarium

Remember, Roman:
To rule the people under law, to establish
The way of peace, to protect the meek,
To battle down the haughty.
These our fine arts, forever.

— Virgil, *The Aeneid*

 nlike the Greeks, the Romans did not question the verities of existence. They very practically made do with what they had, and used their talents to order, pave, build, administer, and control. From a small city-state on the fringes of Hellenic civilization, they rose, through good civil administration, a potent military organization, and fierce patriotism, to conquer the older and more sophisticated civilizations around them. If the Western world still bears a Roman stamp, it is not because the Romans could measure like the Babylonians, ponder like the Greeks, or explore like the Phoenicians. It is because they could, for over seven hundred years, levy taxes to the penny, govern large lands efficiently, and defeat any standing army on the field.

Rome's greatest talent, however, was probably that of assimilation. When she conquered, as she did so often, she made her new subjects not slaves, but partners. At the time of her greatest expansion, around A.D. 150, Rome could count Egyptians, Greeks, Germans, Celts, Persians, and Africans as citizens of her empire. They were just that — citizens of Rome, free to vote for their local leaders, worship their local gods, and follow local pursuits.

We do know how the Babylonians counted, the Greeks thought, the Phoenicians sailed, because they were made children of Rome; and Rome, though demanding and occasionally cruel, allowed them the liberty to be themselves while in her household. Their cultures survived under Roman rule, just as their books were stored in shining libraries paid for by Roman treasuries. Roman practicality, until it was poisoned by wealth and a mad, decayed Imperium, insisted that it was better to convert defeated enemies than destroy them.

So it is with the word *calendar* itself, practicality personified. Romans paid their bills on the first day of

every month[3]; on that day, accountants gathered together in the public squares, toting the heavy books in
which they tabulated the interest that had accrued on
their clients' debts during the month. Calendarium was
the name given to these books. Remittance days being
unpleasant but vital to Roman citizens, the name soon
was used to describe the general system of marking important events of the year.

Roman legend attributed the first calendar to Romulus,
the founder of the city. Like most ancient calendars, it
was based on cycles of the moon, and presented a year
of ten months, starting with March (Romans celebrated
their New Year at the time of the vernal equinox) and
ending in December. The first four months of the year
were named for gods or their attributes and are still easily
recognizable: Martius (March), Aprilis (April), Maius
(May), Junius (June).

Oddly, the Romans then resorted to a stolid numer-
ical scheme for naming the remaining months: Quintilis
(later July), Sextilis (later August), September, October,
November, and December. Six of the months had 30
days, and four had 31, totaling a year of 304 days: 61 days
short of the actual solar year.

---

[3]Modern renters can see that not much has really changed in the
world.

The Romans made up for this gap by means of a macabre custom. Rather than proceeding to March after the official year ended in December, they inserted sixty days into the calendar. This period of time, the coldest and darkest of the year, when the world seemed dead, bore no name. Sixty nameless days — a custom almost inconceivable to the modern mind.

Simple terror gives us an explanation. The Romans lived in fear of horrible beings: lemures, the ghosts of the unhappy dead — purveyors of pestilence and death, witherers of the fields, blood drinkers. Winter was their time, and they had to be supplicated. During their reign, Romans roamed the streets covered in ashes and purified themselves by leaping through sacred fires to avoid the contagion of the vengeful dead. And since calling a spirit by name was sure to attract its frightful attention, these sere months of the lemures' dominion went nameless.[4]

Here we find something common in ancient times: a period of time that is, literally, out of time, given over to private worship, meditation, and to some degree, fear. Although the modern world will allow for no such

---

[4]When European explorers first discovered the island of Madagascar, they noticed ghostly creatures with orbed eyes peering out at them from the gloom of the jungle. They named them after the old Roman ghosts, and the beautiful primates of Madagascar are still called lemurs.

cessation of everyday business, hints of it remain, as we shall see, in observances like Lent.

According to the delightful if dubious historian Livy, Rome's second king, Numa Pompilius (715–673 B.C.) shrugged off the fear that struck his subjects during the winter and used the terror time to create two new months. Perhaps to offset this regal temerity, Numa named the first month after father Janus, the greatest of gods, and piously gave the second a name that reflected the rites performed during it: Februarius, which roughly translates into "to cleanse by sacrifice." Thus January and February entered the calendar, creating the twelve-month year used ever since in the West.

Now things get very confused indeed. Numa shifted the new year from March to January, a reform that would be inflicted on the calendar intermittently for the next few thousand years but would never really stick until the dawn of the modern world. Since the Romans also had a terror of even numbers[5], Numa added days to several of the even-numbered months. January, now the first month, had to be lucky and was given an extra day. February was left with an even number of days; since it was given

---

[5]A Roman prejudice that survives today among the Italians, who know that placing an even number of coffee beans in a glass of Sambuca or olives in a martini will violate the fundamental laws of the universe.

over to the unhappy dead, the Romans thought this appropriate. Numa's new system allowed the year of twelve months to have 355 days: an uneven, lucky number.

Luck and ill-intending spirits, beneficent numbers and days to simply pray: early Roman society was delirious with superstition, augury, and religious theater. The Romans filled their calendar with religious festivals: the Meditrinalia, the Lupercal, the Saturnalia, and the Floralia, to list but a few. A goddess held sway over a stream and a god over the bridge that spanned it; goddesses watched over fertility, plenty, prosperity, good luck, flowers blooming in the spring, leaves fluttering in the fall. Every grove had its titular deity, every day its presiding spirit, every human act its attending daemon. There was even a god of mildew. The Romans never lost this quality; even after cynical emperors proclaimed themselves gods and the marketing of religion became a glut, the Romans remained a people who, according to the great satirist Petronius, "could meet a god on every street."

The Roman calendar went through very little change over the next six hundred years. By the first century B.C., the year still contained 355 days, and was still based on the cycles of the moon. Rome, however, had spent that time consolidating control over the Italian peninsula, the Mediterranean, and finally, most of the Middle East. She had become not simply an empire, but the first world power to emerge in the West since the conquests of Alexander. By the end of the first millennium B.C., her only conceivable military rival was distant China, too far away to pose a threat.

Julian calendar, Byzantine era.

The mistress of the world, as her fervent propagandists called Rome, still used an ancient lunar calendar based on a religion of farmers and Bronze Age warriors. Still piously observed by citizens and dutifully sponsored by the state, the Roman religious calendar nonetheless held too many inconsistencies to be effective in the very serious business of running the world. The Romans now had an empire to administer; and that demanded precision.

As necessary as the moon was for keeping track of religious observances, its use presented great practical difficulties, especially when it came to determining the extent of the true, solar year. The problem was one of simple mathematics: one solar year, one circuit of earth around the sun, lasts for 365 days, while a lunar month lasts for (roughly) 29 days. Twelve of those months together make up 348 days — short of the solar year by seventeen days. Numa had probably realized this shortfall when he added extra days to the calendar here and there, but even after his reforms, the Roman year still fell short of the solar year by about ten days.

Why was this important? Why did the human year have to coordinate with the year carved out by the sun? The answer lies in agriculture, the economic basis of the ancient world. Assume for a moment that you are a Roman farmer in the year 100 B.C. You know that your seed should be planted at the time of the vernal equinox to ensure a September harvest. Now assume, for the sake of argument, that the equinox falls on the correct solar date, March 22. Sure enough, the end of summer yields a superb crop. The next year, you prepare to sow again. But this is the 355-day calendar, and counting one year from the last equinox makes this one fall on March 11. So it goes for the next several years, until by 95 B.C., the calendar instructs you to commit an absurdity and plant your seeds in midwinter.

Luckily for Rome, her farmers ignored the calendar, trusting instead their close observation of the stars, the angle of the sun, migrating birds, and the thousand other natural changes that occur when the seasons turn. Gradually, even the magistrates of the growing empire realized that the calendar was very seriously flawed.

The simple answer to these problems would have been recognition that lunar and the solar calendar systems simply do not fit. Romans being Romans, however — traditional and stubborn — their astrologers tried to force them to fit for centuries, with results so excruciating they need not be explored. The lunar system should have been done away with, but it had become so vital to the ritual calendar of the republic that the Romans simply could not abandon it. The calendar, then, in spite of occasional frantic adjustments, gradually fell out of sync with the seasons it was supposed to chart. By 50 B.C. the vernal equinox, which should occur around March 20, fell on the Ides of May, May 15. The equinox was a cornerstone of Roman agrarian life; it signaled the start of the spring planting season, a vital signpost of the agricultural year. The fact that it now fell in mid-May was simply untenable. Clearly, something had to be done.

Something was done, and by none other than Julius Caesar, a man who solved problems with dispatch.

Caesar (100–44 B.C.) was one of history's most remarkable figures. After spending a dissolute youth as the favored son of a prominent Roman family, he decided at the age of thirty to conquer Rome while it was conquering the world. After a political career filled with intrigues, allegiances, and betrayals, stunning military campaigns and a bloody civil war, he succeeded.

After he became the undisputed master of the Roman world, Caesar surprised both friends and enemies by proving no mere brute. He pardoned most of his enemies, balanced the Roman budget, provided new parks and amphitheaters for the common people, and vowed to strengthen the tottering republic.

Caesar even turned his attention to the calendar. He invited Sosigenes, an Alexandrian astronomer, to transform the dilapidated system into a model of calendrical efficiency. Sosigenes took Caesar at his word and chose the revolutionary method of utterly abandoning the lunar system and basing the Roman year on the sun. The more traditional Roman priests shrieked at this scientific blasphemy, but they had not seen anything yet. Sosigenes decided that before he could truly amend the calendar, he had to get the year back into natural sync with the sun. His sudden, dramatic reform in 44 B.C., which never would have been possible in conservative

Rome had it not borne the imprimatur of Caesar, passed into Roman history as "the Long Year."

Sosigenes introduced two intercalations, or breaks in the calendar. He inserted thirty uncounted days into the middle of February and another thirty-five between the last day of November and the first day of December. In other words, February 2 would pass, a normal day. The next thirty days, by decree, would be uncounted; days literally out of time. On the thirty-first day, criers would stroll the streets, announcing that today was February 3. The tale of days would begin again. The Romans endured this jarring intercalation because Caesar insisted that it was the right, the Roman, thing to do. When all was said and done, sixty-seven days had been added to the year. The Long Year, indeed: 44 B.C. lasted for 432 days.

Caesar must have been pleased; he liked ruffling feathers, and he liked things that worked. Sosigenes had calculated the length of the year at 365 days and 6 hours and set a calendar that accurately measured it. Sosigenes did not, however, reckon with the fact that the year is, in fact, 365 days, *5 hours, and 49 minutes long*. While these extra eleven minutes a year might not seem to amount to much, over the millennia the calendar, losing that small bundle of time each year, inevitably began to pull the date of the equinox back toward New Year's Day. This small error would have great future consequences.

Had he lived into old age, Caesar might well have hired another astronomer to tell him just this, to tweak the calendar just that little bit and ensure that it kept up with the sun.

Had he lived. Caesar died during the Long Year, the year he had created. On March 15 of A.D. 44, despite the warnings of friends and prophets, he ventured from his home and into the dangerous streets, where many enemies waited. Some hated the tyrant who spoke of liberty; others hated the libertine who had become a moralist; most simply hated the man. He was trapped and cornered and killed, drawing his toga over his face that he might not behold the striking arms of friends. His death brought about another civil war, another national spasm of suffering, agony, and death, ensuring that the Long Year was so named in Roman memory not only for its added days.

Even as Rome came to dominate the Mediterranean, it faced an age-old enemy on a vital border. Throughout the lands north of the Italian peninsula, scores of barbarian tribes, serving a multitude of neighborhood warlords, vied with one another for land and treasure. This was true internecine warfare, for the conflicting tribes were cultural siblings: they shared religious beliefs, spoke dialects of the same language, and enjoyed a singular, mystical vision of the universe. The Romans called them Gauls. Alexander had encountered and admired them years before, when they were already known among the Greeks by the name they still carry: Keltoi — the Celts.

Although Celtic civilization would be subsumed by Rome, it never really died, and it introduced a new music into the dance of the year. Caesar had given the world a calendar of order and precision, marked by rigorous timekeeping. By classical times, Roman festivals celebrated a well-regulated universe, based on astronomy, affairs of state, and benevolent, predictable deities.

In the Celts, the Romans discovered a people at once vigorous, macabre, romantic, and doleful: a people who, in defeat, changed their conquerors.

The Celts brought to the orderly Roman calendar a unique division of the year, based not on the solstices and equinoxes but on the rhythms of human and animal life. They celebrated feasts inspired not by distant gods but by the surrounding natural world. They introduced an atavistic poetry into the calendar, which, during celebrations like Halloween or May Day, still resonates in the modern world. Most importantly, the Celts transformed Caesar's practical timepiece into a mystical reiteration of life's journey. Rome, queen of civilizations and mistress of the world, made time obey her need for precision. The fact that the calendar, in the end, is an observance not of time but of timelessness is a gift of the barbarians.

CHAPTER FOUR

A Day and a Night

The way they dress is astonishing. They wear brightly colored and embroidered shirts; with trousers called brachae and cloaks fastened at the shoulder with a brooch. . . . They are very tall in stature, with rippling muscles under clear white skin. Their hair is blond, but not naturally so: they bleach it, to this day, artificially, washing it with lime and combing it back from their foreheads. . . . Their aspect is terrible to behold. . . . They look like wood-demons.

— Diodorus

 he Greek historian Diodorus's wide-eyed description of a typical Celt gives us a good idea of what most Greeks and Romans thought of their eerie northern neighbors. The Celts were warriors and herdsmen, tribal folk who lived in ringed hill forts amid the precious cattle that sustained them. We know little about their origins, although it is certain that they shared ancient ancestry with other Indo-European peoples like the Greeks and Romans.

While their distant relations were spreading into the Mediterranean basin, the Celts moved northwest, crossing the Danube into recorded history sometime around 1000 B.C. Over the next five hundred years, they colonized most of Europe. Although their greatest concentration lay in the rich fields and fertile river valleys of modern France, the Celts established settlements as far west as Spain (where the province of Galatia still carries an echo of their name) and as far north as Scotland and Ireland.

Although primitive by classical standards, the Celts created a vibrant culture during their time of autonomy, and they lived well. They brewed beer, loved wine, and discovered the secret of brandy. They enjoyed feasts of grilled venison and wild boar, at which their skilled musicians (so skilled that Celtic musical tutors were sought throughout the ancient world) sang of heroes, battle, and love. They were also superb metalsmiths; Celtic swords, in fact, fetched top dollar in Rome.

Nor did the Celts make only weaponry. They could shape iron, tin, and bronze into everyday utensils of delicate beauty. The artifacts that survive give us a window into the Celtic imagination: a magnificent cauldron on which animals and gods sport in high relief; a delicate bronze flagon with a green dragon forming its twining handle and a bright-eyed duckling resting on its spout, so fey and vigorous, one could easily imagine it hoisted by one of Tolkien's dwarves; lovely figurines of sinuous, playful deer. These pieces, more primitive but somehow more welcoming than the severe perfection of classical art, reveal much of their long-dead creators: a love of life, a deep affection for nature, and an energetic, humorous disposition.

Although they did not develop a written language, the Celts had a rich oral tradition of lore and wisdom passed down through their bards and their priestly caste, known to the Romans — and hence to history — as the druids, from a Latin word meaning "wizard."

The druids led the Celts in worship of nature. They knelt to limnetic gods beside quiet pools and bowed before twisted oaks in misty groves, listening for the whispers of the gods through the rustling leaves. They also asked questions of the severed heads of defeated enemies, which they kept preserved in oil. Theirs was a religion of magic and moonlight and dread, but also one of democratic ideals: a central tenet of Celtic belief insisted that all men and women were equal creatures under one god.

Unlike the misogynistic Greeks and Romans, the Celts loved women, and were rather awed by their quiet strength and eternal mystery. Celtic women had equal voices in all major decisions. There is, in fact, compelling evidence that the chief deity of the Celts was a goddess who had many forms, and changed as the year changed.

The Celts loved change, transformation, shape-shifting. In an old Irish myth, the hero sings of his many aspects:

> I am the wind on the sea,
> The ocean wave
> And the roar it makes.
> I am the Bull of Seven Fights,
> a vulture on a cliff.
> I am a drop of dew
> and the fairest of flowers.
> I am a bold boar,
> a salmon in a pool.
> I am a lake upon a plain.
> I am the word of power,
> The point of the sword:
> I am the god who fires the blade.

To the Roman mind, this would have seemed the most primitive kind of boasting. They did not know enough of the Celts to understand that, in the Celtic mind, the division between god and mortal, life and death, darkness and light, indeed, between any one thing and another, was a matter of mere perception. Just as a lump of metal shaped by clever hands could become a delicate brooch gleaming between a lover's breasts, so too could any common thing — a man, an animal, a puff of breeze — shape itself into something remarkable: a god, a spirit-guide, a divine voice.

They were in love with the night, calling themselves "the children of darkness," and they measured days from sundown to sundown. The Roman historian Tacitus, in a famous passage, remarks that the Germans (who used the same system of daily measurement as the Celts) "do not reckon like us, by days, but by nights." Celts regarded the night with deep reverence, and held all of their great festivals after the sun went down.

To the Celtic mind, the dark of night was felt to be nearer the other world, the land of ghosts and fairies, witches and magical beings, than the light of day. People born after the fall of dark were widely considered to have the second sight, that is, to be able to see phantoms. Fairies and other creatures became active only after sunset. Night belonged to them, and to intrude on their realm was risky business. Mortals should withdraw to their firesides as soon as the sun set. Throwing out water or fireside ashes in the dark was considered especially risky, lest the dead, who visited the home between ten and twelve o'clock, should be disturbed.

The Celts also had an ephemeral, almost oriental notion of time. The quote that supplied the title of this chapter comes from an ancient Irish legend in which the hero, Mac Oc, is promised possession of the god Dagda's hostel, or hill fort, for one day and one night. When Dagda returns the next day to find Mac Oc still in residence and orders him out, he is rebuffed with that simple, seemingly nonsensical explanation: of a day and a night, all the world is made. In the myth, Dagda instantly sees the truth of this statement, and Mac Oc retains possession of the fort.

The Celts regarded this kind of thinking, so absurd to the analytical mind, as an expression of the deepest wisdom; in fact, they seem to have based their calendar on the very notion that one day holds within its brief confines all the elements of the entire year, and that conversely, the year — indeed all of eternity — is simply one long day in the dreaming mind of God.

In 1896 a Gaulish calendar of the year was discovered at Coligny, France. Although translated into a Roman idiom, the calendar gives us great insight into Celtic concepts of calendrical time.

Like the day, the Celtic year was divided into two halves, a dark half and a light half, also called winter and summer halves. Fittingly, given the Celtic fondness for darkness, the year began with the dark half, on the first of November, a Celtic festival called Samhain, literally meaning "the end of summer." The light half of the year began six months later, on Beltane, the first of May.

We will explore both of these festivals at length during our journey through the year. The important thing to note here is that they demonstrate a genuine departure from the customary Mediterranean method of reckoning, based as it was on solstice and equinox. For many

Celtic calendar discovered in Coligny, France, 1896.

years, scholars wondered why the Celts bisected their year on the first days of November and May, rather than in December and June, as did the Greeks, Romans, and Semitic peoples. The answer came in the late nineteenth century, and was worried over at length by James George Frazer in his masterpiece *The Golden Bough*:

> These dates coincide with none of the four great hinges on which the solar year revolves, to wit, the solstices and equinoxes. Yet the first of May and the first of November mark turning points of the year in Europe. The one ushers in the genial heat and the rich vegetation of summer, the other heralds, if it does not share, the cold barrenness of winter. These particular points of the year, while they are of little moment to the European husbandman (farmer), deeply concern the herdsman; for it is on the approach of summer that he drives his cattle out into the fields to crop on the fresh grass, and it is on the approach of winter that he leads them back to the shelter and safety of the stall.

Although by classical times the Celts had learned some very sophisticated and effective agricultural techniques and no longer relied solely on their cattle for sustenance, the ancient calendar, which they had probably developed during the Stone Age as they wandered with their herds over the eastern steppes, continued to mark the passage of their year.

Two more feasts quartered the year: one on February 1 and the other on August 1. Because these observances were based not on astronomy but on animals and their ways, on forage and pasture, and on minute observation of slow-changing nature, they introduced to the world not just a new method of reckoning days but a new way of experiencing time.

A mythology grew up around these festival days that reflected the Celtic notion that nature was, in the final reckoning, a feminine creature; a goddess who, in keeping with the Celtic fondness for metamorphosis, changed as the seasons changed.

Beginning the year at Samhain as a shriveled crone, the goddess was reborn on February 1 as a beautiful maiden who would grow into the fullness of her beauty by May Day. As the summer waxed, so did the goddess, celebrating her marriage to the male god Cernunnos (usually depicted with stag horns) at the beginning of August. Their marriage guaranteed the future, for no sooner was the divine wedding night concluded than the year began to wane, the goddess to age. By November, she, with the world, had shrunken again into her dotage; but the child she carried from her marriage to Cernunnos was, in fact, herself — ready to be reborn after winter's darkness.

Here we find a goddess possessed of no personality but that of the earth: changing and, though unyielding in her change, never unfair. She suffers with the world of her dominion, ages, and, like doting human parents, is reborn through her power of procreation. She is as mortal as her worshippers. She knows that she is winter and its death, spring and its dissolution, summer and its fall. While sophisticated Romans slaughtered lambs in honor of philandering Jupiter and draped purple robes of homage over statues of shrill, vengeful Juno, their barbaric northern enemies made Woman the apotheosis of earth's mutable beauties.

The Celts dominated Europe for five centuries, creating their lovely, antic flagons and their long shining swords, singing songs to the rising sun and the glowing moon, worshipping water, women, and wine. Although they were warriors, terrible in battle and never forgetting slight or quarrel, they loved the world and all of its beauties and were happily afraid of nothing but the sky falling on their heads. Then Caesar came, and the sky fell.

When they were not fighting one another, the Celts turned their considerable martial energy toward Rome. In spite of the fact that trade was active and often friendly between Celtic Europe and the Mediterranean (the Celts traded their precious amber and valuable swords for the Greek and Roman wine that they loved to drink but could not hope to duplicate), Greeks and Romans considered the Celts pure barbarians.[6] They had good reasons; Celtic intrusions into the Mediterranean basin left smoking fields, burning towns, and bitter memories.

---

[6]A wonderful onomatopoeic word from Greco-Roman civilization, *barbarian* referred to those people who could not speak real tongues, but instead went, "ba-ba-ba," like sheep or other animals.

Rome itself was sacked by a Celtic horde in 390. The proud Romans had to bribe the Celts to head back north with an enormous gift from the treasury — a humiliation the Romans never forgot or forgave, and which eventually led to the destruction of Celtic liberty.

The Celts achieved their victories over more organized foes not through superior tactics (they had no tactics to speak of) but through the sheer barbaric terror of their attack. Like the Bronze Age heroes of Homer's epics (to whom they were distantly related), they rode to war on rumbling chariots, first hurling their long spears at the enemy and then, at the point of contact, vaulting down to engage in hand-to-hand combat. Diodorus gives us a few more hair-raising details: "Some wear bronze helmets with figures picked out on them, even horns, which make them look even taller than they already are; others cover themselves with breast-armor made from chains. Most, however, are content with the weapons nature has given them, and rush naked into battle. Weird, discordant horns are sounded, and they shout in chorus with their deep and harsh voices, beating their swords in a rhythm against their shields."

On one famous occasion in 273 B.C., marauding Celts defeated a highly disciplined Greek phalanx at Delphi. Afterward they sacked the temple, the holiest of Greek shrines. This act of bloody sacrilege sent shock waves through the Greco-Roman world. By Caesar's time, Celtic raids on the border were growing more frequent;

something had to be done. In 58 B.C., a decade before he developed the calendar that would bear his name, Caesar set out with 360,000 men to conquer Celtic Europe.

He nearly succeeded. Although they vastly outnumbered the Romans, the Gauls, mutually suspicious and too independent for their own good, never formed an alliance strong enough to repel the invaders. In an attritive nine-year war, Caesar destroyed his splintered foes tribe by tribe. By the time he famously crossed the Rubicon to become master of the empire, Caesar had planted Roman standards from the Alps to the English Channel, made most of modern France a Roman province, and even led a brief reconnaissance into Britain.

In A.D. 43, during the reign of the emperor Claudius, Roman triremes braved the choppy English Channel and invaded Britain, where they conquered as far north as the Scottish lowlands. Here they encountered the Picts, a particularly hostile branch of the Celtic family who painted themselves blue before roaring into battle and coated their hair with lime to make it stand on end.[7] The Romans foresaw blood and treasure lost in the dreadful Caledonian glens, and wisely, under the emperor Hadrian, erected the wall that stretches across the vaulting North Umbrian countryside. Much of the wall

---

[7]"Pict" is the name that the Romans gave these people, from the Latin word for paint. We still use it when we admire pictures in museums.

is still there, guarded now not by centurions but by shepherds, who drive their bleating flocks along the precise imperial latitude at which Rome recognized her limit.

Across the conquered lands, never far behind the triumphant legions, came Roman colonists, building roads and aqueducts, commanding the locals to speak the Latin tongue and worship Roman gods, founding settlements that became cities. It seemed that Europe was destined to become and remain another distant suburb of Rome.

Over the long centuries, however, something happened that not even canny Caesar could have guessed: the Celts whom he defeated, whom his followers subjugated, taxed, educated, and assimilated, outlasted the Eternal City. Although it adopted many Roman ways, Celtic Europe remained at its core tribal and independent. When the last Roman legions marched off to the burning capital of the world in the middle of the fifth century, the Celts, finding themselves again alone, remembered what they had been before the Caesars came.

They were not alone for very long; other tribal peoples from the north and east, never conquered by Rome, came rushing across the ancient empire's borders to fill the sudden cataclysmic vacuum. The Europe that they created would be a mixture of fading memories of Rome and fresh barbaric feuding, and the Celtic sensibility would all but disappear. Except in one place.

A Roman soldier standing on the west coast of

England during the twilight of the empire could at least take pride in the knowledge that at his back lay an entire world wearing the accouterments of Latin civilization. If he could look far enough west, however, he might make out the tiny leather boats of the Hibernians bobbing off the coast of Ireland. Rome had never invaded the small green island on the verges of the western ocean. There the Celts remained, untouched and unhindered, for another four hundred years. Later, as we shall see time and again, when it seemed that so many of the ancient ways had been expunged, Ireland would open her ambered treasury of custom and present the world a long-lost jewel.

On the Continent, the northern barbarians seized the ruins of the empire, only to be conquered in their turn by an earlier conqueror of Rome. This invader fought not with swords but with prayers, and promised as the price of surrender not death or slavery but salvation.

In the early sixth century, a man bearing good news journeyed north from Rome. Named Augustine, he traveled across the dangerous continent and then sailed over the Channel to England. Though a Roman, his good news had nothing to do with the city of Rome, nor with any city of man. He wore neither toga nor breastplate, displayed neither sword nor purple standard. Instead, under simple woolen robes, a crucifix dangled from his neck.

CHAPTER FIVE

Converting the Faithful

European thought is inconceivable except as a dialogue with Christianity.

— Fernand Braudel

he death of Rome took centuries. Civil wars, mad emperors, usurping generals; calamity after calamity shook the ancient empire, now too infirm, corrupted, and nerveless to spring back.

As provincial troops rushed home to quell riots or face down rebellious factions in the army, tribes of Germans and Goths began to push at the now-fragile eastern borders of the empire. At first the Romans made practical use of their perilous situation and recruited troops from the ranks of the barbarians; Goths and Gauls became foot soldiers in the Roman army. Soon they would be generals. It was only a matter of time before these barely romanized, fully militarized soldiers would turn against their masters. The inevitable came in 410, when an army commanded by Alaric the Goth flew into open revolt. After rampaging from Illyria to Italy and crushing every army sent to halt it, Alaric's horde finally appeared before the defenseless gates of the Eternal City.

No enemy had threatened Rome's gates since Hannibal of Carthage, more than six hundred years earlier; no foe had actually penetrated the walls since the Celts in 390 B.C. Alaric had little reverence for Roman tradition, and on a mild April evening, he stormed through the gates and immolated the capital of the world. The last Roman emperor would not abdicate for another forty years, but Alaric's campaign sealed the doom of the Western empire. Although in the East the new capital of Constantinople kept traces of classical civilization alive through the Middle Ages, it was at this point, the old historians used to claim, that the West, devoid now of Rome's precise political and military genius, fell into darkness.

That darkness, we now know, was not all that dark; if it seemed so compared to the glories of Hellenistic civilization, flashes of light from a new empire illuminated it. Although it began as an empire of the spirit, the Christian church, which had become the favored sect of Rome after the sudden, still mysterious conversion of the emperor Constantine in A.D. 321, quickly assumed the powerful trappings of the Roman imperial system.

By A.D. 450, even as barbarians pounded at the gates, the old Roman Empire was swiftly becoming a Catholic parish. Church leaders sent tonsured legions of missionaries deep into the pagan kingdoms. These men and women had to be skillful diplomats as they encountered people of many cultures and faiths settling, usually by brute force, the lands of the old empire. Faced with stubborn, incredulous, and warlike pagans, early missionaries to the north developed an astonishing policy. One example will serve to illustrate the subtlety of their approach to conversion. In the seventh century, Pope Gregory the Great issued a decree to the people of France, who had refused to cease their custom of sacrificing horses at church altars on October 31, the eve of the old Celtic festival Samhain. Gregory's decree reads, in part: "They are no longer to sacrifice beasts to the devil, but they may kill them for food and for the praise of God, and give thanks to the giver of all gifts for his bounty."

A small decree, one of thousands sent out from Rome every year to parishes across Europe; but that one document tells a great tale. Led by pragmatic, clever popes like Gregory, the church seamlessly assimilated pagan feast days into the church calendar, allowing the folk traditions associated with the old holidays to continue, virtually unchanged, under the mantle of the new faith. This is a policy we will meet again and again as we later explore the festivals of the year, as Catholic missionaries spread the word of God not through fire-and-brimstone proselytization, but with a combination of politics, patience, and persuasion.

In places like Ireland, the common people easily adopted the new faith, and Irish Christianity became a luminous marriage of Christian orthodoxy and pagan custom. Beyond Ireland's protected shores, Romano-Celtic civilization had been rapidly subsumed by a new swarm of invaders. These tribes had moved into Europe from the northeast over the long centuries and, though related to the Celts, were more independent, violent, and resilient. They called themselves many different names: Frank, Goth, Saxon, and Lombard. The Roman historian Tacitus had declared them, with justification, to be the greatest fighters in the world; they had inflicted more casualties on Roman troops than any other enemy in history. Year after year, even during the heyday of the empire, Roman senators and emperors rose to voice the same admonishment: We must do something about the Germans.

Beyond the great natural barriers of the Rhine and Danube rivers, in deep forests that were rumored never to have known the light of day, dwelt the Germans. Fiercely resistant to Roman expansion, they were never fully subdued. Intermittent warfare between German and Roman along the great natural frontier of the Rhine lasted until Rome finally caved in on itself, and the Germans stepped forward to claim all of Europe.

Germanic peoples like the fierce Norse, who as Vikings would devastate so much of Europe during the ninth century, had a violent but balefully beautiful mythology. They called the world Midgard, or Middle Earth. Midgard covered seething Niflheim, the land of the dead, like a lid on a cauldron. From that whirling place of dread and torment, ruled by a pale and ghastly hag named Hel, came terrible monsters and vengeful spirits to seek out prey among the living. On the verges of Midgard itself the frost giants dwelt: huge unsightly brutes, the illegitimate children of the gods, who hated men and sent crushing snows and freezing winds to destroy them. But high above, proud and consoling, stood the ramparts of Asgard, the glittering citadel of the Aesir, the gods of the Norse, who left their lofty realm to do battle with the frost giants and the fell creatures of Hel in the wide arena of Midgard.

Chief among the Aesir was Wotan (also called Odin), the All-Father, who rode through the skies on his eight-legged horse Sleipnir, keeping an eye (literally, for he only had one, having lost the other in a trade for wisdom) on his mortal charges below. From time to time Odin wandered the earth disguised as an old man to share his deep knowledge with men; but usually he held forth from his great throne at Asgard, with two great black ravens perched on his shoulders. At Odin's command, they could fly like the wind and bring him back news of all that happened below.

Unlike the Celts, the Norse charted the year by solstice and equinox, and their major feasts fell on Midsummer Day (June 24), when the sun was near its height, and Yule (December 21), when the sun was at its weakest point. The Norse believed that giant wolves pursued the sun through the sky; at these important moments, to aid the sun in his journey, Odin led a wolf hunt through the heavens. Sleipnir's charging hooves stirred rattling thunder and flashing lightning, and the trees shook with the wind of his passage. The Norse called these storms the Wild Hunt, when their gods, led by magnificent Odin, burst out of Asgard to do battle with the enemies of the sun.

Odin's chief warrior, and the most beloved of the Norse gods, was the great Thor, a redheaded, blustering oaf who swung his mighty hammer against the frost giants who threatened humankind. Loud, boorish, and rather stupid, the mighty Thor was (because, not in spite, of these qualities) deeply loved by his worshippers. He rumbled through the sky on a silver chariot drawn by goats, those sturdy friends to the struggling farmer. The clatter of their hooves on the clouds made the thunder that promised rain and drove evil away.

As the church coaxed the Germanic tribes into its embrace, the celebrations of northern paganism were transformed into days of prayer and worship, but many of the ancient customs remained intact, grafted onto a new faith. To this day, many of the notable customs associated with major feasts like Christmas and Easter (and even such seemingly American celebrations like Groundhog Day) find their roots in ancient Teutonic culture. The old pagan ways survived the Catholic conversion through the active encouragement of the missionaries themselves, who were only too happy to allow native practices to continue as long as at some point during the festivities someone consumed a communion wafer.

These early years of the European millennium were marked not simply by the rise of the church, but by the emergence of a new kind of human being: a crea-

Shepherd's calendar, from the Middle Ages.

ture neither Latin nor Celtic, neither Greek nor German, but somehow a combination of all of these things.

In the old Roman province of Gaul, the people named themselves and their country after their barbarian, not Roman, forebears, the Franks, and gradually rolled their spoon-fed Latin into the soft backs of their mouths to create musical French. The Anglo-Saxons conquered Celtic England by modeling their primitive military on the regiments and legions of Rome; their English descendants still do. Norse converts to Christianity praised the birth of their new god Jesus by igniting fir trees, just as their pagan neighbors immolated trees for Thor. Millennia later, lights shining on Christmas trees serve as gentle reminders of these wild rites.

An astonishing artifact from the seventh century reveals this society in transition. It is a mold, the kind used in making cheap amulets, trinkets such as holy tourists to places like Lourdes or Fatima still buy. The mold holds two side-by-side impressions. One is carved into the shape of a small "t," and was obviously used to cast a crucifix. The other, sitting inches away, forms a capital "T": a representation of the hammer of Thor. In addition to his other duties, Thor was also the protector of merchants, who, in the seventh century, finding their customers torn between the old god of the north and the new god from the south, shrewdly took advantage of both markets.

Nowhere can this marriage of cultures be seen

more clearly than in the names of the days of the week. The Romans, isolated on the Italian peninsula, had developed an eight-day week based on market days, but legionnaires stationed throughout the Mediterranean soon picked up the oriental habit of seven-day counting and brought it back to Rome. By the time of Constantine, the seven-day week had become the standard.

As Roman Christianity spread into Germanic Europe, fresh converts to the faith adopted the seven-day week. The new church remarkably allowed several of the old pagan names to remain attached to their days, and they still reflect the mixed society that created them.

Sunday, the first day of the week, retained the ancient name of the father of the father of the gods, wellspring of all life and the bringer of all good things: the sun.

Next comes the great mistress, chief lamp of dark night, she who makes us love, dream, wander, quarrel, and forgive, who blesses the night with alabaster gleam. Monday is the day of the moon.

The next four days of the week are named after Nordic gods and goddesses. Tyre, the god of fertility, rules Tuesday, "Tyre's day." Tyre brings the soft rain, rules the mists, and cares for the woman groaning in both passion and birth. Wednesday is named after Wotan, the all-father, ruler of the nine worlds, giver of wisdom, defender of man. Thursday still carries the name of mighty Thor, he of the hammer and the thunderbolt. Friday

71

honors Freya, Odin's faithful wife and the queen of the gods.

Saturday hearkens all the way back to Rome: Saturn's day, on which the world may rest in honor of the ancient father of all the gods.

Catholic rule in Europe created a phantasmagoria of colorful festivals, half pagan, half Christian, that measured the processes of life and culled the subtleties of the seasons from the larger year. Each feast reached back into deep antiquity and, thanks to the politics of the early church, had been successfully reinterpreted in a Christianized context. The conversion of the myriad pagan tribes only took about two centuries; its result, a politically fragmented but religiously united Catholic Europe, lasted for almost a thousand years.

In peasant villages across Europe, parish priests became unquestioned leaders in both spiritual and practical affairs. Higher up the social ladder, cardinals dined with princes, hatching military campaigns and political plots. At the pinnacle of worldly power, even kings recognized (but often chafed against) the supreme authority of the Roman pope; and it was a pope, not a king, who sent thousands of young men off to the greatest societal endeavor in medieval history, the Crusades. By the early sixteenth century, the church had enjoyed almost ten centuries of hegemony over the Western world.

Those millennia of rule had made the church proud,

arrogant, and increasingly despised. The Great Schism of the fourteenth century, during which two rival popes, seated in different countries, vied for power, seriously tarnished the reputation of the papacy. Kings, weary of kowtowing to Rome, began to test the secular strength of the church by taxing or confiscating church lands within their realms. The church fought back by becoming more pompous, panoplied, and arrogant. Priests urged their parishioners to buy indulgences, guarantees of a lessened term in purgatory, a practice that made the public even more cynical and disgusted. In response to the growing criticism, the church finally declared that the pope was an infallible vessel of God's will, and that any practice of the church sanctioned by the bishop of Rome had to be accepted as a prerequisite of faith. By the dawn of the modern world, the church had become, in essence, a spiritual dictatorship.

In 1517, an angry, spiritually tormented Augustine monk walked up to the doors of a church in Wittenberg, Germany. He removed three items from his *sabertache:* a hammer, a nail, and a list of ninety-five grievances leveled against the Roman Catholic Church. The friar nailed his manifesto to the church doors. The clang of his hammer would soon reverberate throughout Europe.

Martin Luther, the father of the Reformation, helped to create a new kind of Christianity. Protestantism, so named because of its roots in protest against the church, gave prime importance to individual faith, and to each individual's personal relationship with the savior. Rejecting what they saw as the empty ritualizing of the church, Luther and his followers pointed out that most of the church's customs and holy days came from the pagan past. They accused the church itself of being a pagan institution, and vehemently condemned the celebrations of the ecclesiastical year. Years of heated accusations led to a rising hysteria among Protestants against any and all things that smelled remotely pagan.

After Luther, a generation of new reformers emerged, who followed the precise but terrifying teachings of John Calvin. Calvin claimed that faith alone is a guarantee of salvation, and that human beings are predetermined from birth to achieve salvation or to be forever damned. Calvin's followers introduced a new militancy into the Protestant movement. They rejected any representation of divinity sculpted or painted by the hand of man, rejected ceremony, ritual, festival, and feast — remnants, they claimed, of a sordid pagan past embalmed by corrupt Rome. They set out to smash the icons in their frames, to cast the gilded statues from their pedestals, to purify the world in preparation for the second coming of Christ. Instead of ushering in the New Jerusalem, they brought about a societal change that would transform both Europe and the newly discovered American continents and threaten with extinction many ancient customs and festivals: the rise of the Puritan.

CHAPTER SIX

Empty Pockets

I am Raftery the poet, full of hope and love,
With sightless eyes and undistracted calm
On my long journey westward, by the light of my heart,
Weak and tired to the end of my road.
Look at me now, my back to the wall,
Singing my songs to empty pockets.

— Owen Raftery
"Raftery's Reply"

he attempted destruction of Catholic Europe by reformers like Luther and Calvin partially succeeded. German rulers, eager to become independent of Rome, protected and encouraged the Protestants, and the movement spread throughout northern Europe. In England, Henry VIII cynically broke from the church so that he could divorce his wife

Catherine of Aragon, who had unconscionably refused to bear him a male heir. Henry then seized the monasteries and systematically despoiled them, hauling the accrued wealth of five centuries — books and paintings, statuary and gold — back to his treasury. Henry's royal larceny was repeated throughout Europe, until only France, Spain, and Italy remained resolutely Catholic, enclaves of the old church surrounded by countries in the grip of a spiritual revolution.

During the years of the Protestant ascent in the sixteenth and seventeenth centuries, Europe and England succumbed to the notion that all things inspired by ancient mythologies had to be expunged. In villages throughout Europe, many women still practiced superstitious forms of healing and divination handed down through the generations from the pagan days of the Romans. These folk practices now bore the stamp of witchcraft. A hysteria spread through the continent, as Protestant ministers preached against the evil of the witch and the warlock. Soon old women who healed children's fevers with herbs gathered by moonlight found themselves bound to burning stakes.

The beleaguered Roman Catholic Church launched a Counter-Reformation, during which it violently tried to purge itself of all things pagan. Soon the most accomplished witch-hunters and torturers proved to be Catholic priests, whose church had, so many centuries earlier, won over the hearts and minds of Europe by allowing their parishioners to dance at May Day and light bonfires at Halloween.

Another force of thought countervailed these driven servants of a pious God. During the sixteenth century, a new mentality began to infuse European civilization. Old ways of thinking were increasingly challenged by men who tinkered with the new notion that the world — indeed, the universe — was measurable and predictable, not merely the enchanted, sometimes blighted plaything of a beneficent but unpredictable god. They placed their faith in the rational mind of man, and began to explore the world around using reason, logic, and observation. These men, the first real scientists, took all of nature as their study, and their discoveries in astronomy, chemistry, physics, and medicine changed the world. No aspect of nature escaped their purview, and their research revealed such wonders as the fact that the earth orbits the sun (not the other way around) and that blood circulates through the human body like a swift river. Along the way, they even took note of the calendar.

The strength of the Julian calendar needs no more testament than the simple fact that, 1,500 years after its creator had perished; after the empire he fathered had collapsed, barbarian kingdoms risen and fallen, and Europe been born in long centuries of blood and iron; even after a cultural renaissance had awakened the sleeping mind of science in the West; after all of this,

Caesar's calendar still measured the year. But it did so, by now, poorly. Because of Sosigenes' ancient, eleven-minute-a-year lapse, by 1530 the vernal equinox fell on March 10 — a full nine days behind the sun.

The equinox was as important to medieval society as it had been to Roman. Farmers used it to calculate the exact date of Easter, and the beginning of the liturgical year, and all of the other major holy days were calculated from this date. These feasts, far from being simple days of worship, also told farmers when to plant and sow their crops, when harvest should commence, when winter began. Keeping Easter in tune with the equinox was a vital necessity; and it was no longer being done by Caesar's old calendar.

In a great irony of history, the astronomers who recognized the calendar's flaw called for its reform and found their champion in none other than a Roman pope. Pope Gregory XIII was anxious to rid the church of its superstitious past, and he eagerly invited the leading astronomers in Europe to come to Rome and reform the wayward calendar. In 1582, after months of argument and calculation, Pope Gregory XIII's guests presented him with the modern calendar. In a papal bull dated March 1, 1582, the pope announced his stunning reform.

To restore the civil year to a correspondence with the astronomical year, Gregory, much as Caesar had done fifteen hundred years before him (and in the same city!) lopped nine days out of the calendar in one fell blow, ordering that the October 5, 1582 become the fifteenth. To ensure that the year would continue to keep up with the sun, he also decreed that every year whose number is not divisible by four would consist of 365 days, and that every year divisible by four, but not divisible by one hundred, would have 366 days. That extra day every four years would serve to restore those pesky eleven minutes slipping out of the Julian calendar every year. These became known as leap years, because during them the orderly sequence of days would "leap" by one extra day.

Gregory's calendar is still used throughout the Western world. Solar in reckoning, it keeps an exact tally of the years, needing to be tweaked only occasionally back into alignment with our star by "leap seconds." The Roman calendar, modified but essentially that of old Julius, still keeps rein on the wandering sun.

Protestant countries were slow in adopting what they considered a papist (and therefore soiled) calendar. England, in fact, did not adopt the Gregorian reforms until 1732 — an extraordinary example of prejudice defeating reason. Like their active disdain of the old festivals, the Puritans also enjoyed a distinct distaste for anything that emanated from the maw of Rome, even if it made common sense. Ideology now condemned both religion and science. Puritan England also proved so hostile to the annual rites of the year that even wildly popular celebrations like May Day and Halloween began to die out.

Then something happened on the round world; it was found to be so. In October 1492, a man named Columbus landed on the shores of what he took to be Cathay. He was dead wrong, but he gave citizens of the Old World, their traditions threatened and fading, a way of escape. On the shores of North America, English colonists, even Puritans, would slough off the shackles of their past and create a new society (and ultimately a new country), based on ideas of self-determination and individual liberty.

The immigrants who came to America during the three centuries after Columbus made a world in which they could not be imprisoned for their religious practices or beliefs, in which no inquisitor could question their folkways, no king or pope reach across the wide Atlantic to strangle their right to be themselves. Many nations sent their children to the Americas; of the new lives they would forge here, one can serve to tell the larger tale.

Owen Raftery, whose lament prefaces this chapter, was a blind Irish poet of the eighteenth century who lived through calamitous times. He grew up, and then old, in a country suffering a brutal foreign occupation. Sporadic rebellions against the English failed around him, and the final vestiges of Celtic Ireland seemed dead by the time that Raftery, late in the century, drew his last breath.

Raftery knew that the last of traditional Ireland had been crushed to the point of extinction by wave after wave of English invasion. The English had led sporadic invasions into Ireland from the time of Elizabeth I, but the culture of the land itself had always survived: its music and stories, its unique form of Christianity, in which old gods and goddesses were worshipped as saints, its poetic language and its casual love of life's simple pleasures.

In the mid-seventeenth century, the English Puritan Oliver Cromwell, who despised Catholics, despised the Irish, and despised Irish Catholics with a fury that can only be described as pathological, invaded the island. His men leveled every castle they could find, burned every town, and killed whole counties.

After his crushing campaign, Cromwell established a system of so-called Penal Laws, a stringent codification of his own prejudices that made it illegal for the Irish to openly take communion, or pray to the saints, or teach the native tongue — even to sing and dance in the traditional Irish manner.

Now, more than one hundred years later, Raftery saw another futile rebellion ending in death, sorrow, and the destruction of the culture of his fathers. His famous lament seems not only a personal cry of despair, but also a last spasm of the broken Celtic heart.

*   *   *

The Ireland whose cultural decline Raftery lamented would soon face a more practical calamity — the potato famine of 1848–50. During the famine, some million Irish peasants died of starvation: an equal number sailed away to the New World. But long before that disaster, from countries all over a Europe still dominated by monarchs and divided between an indolent aristocracy and a toiling poor, people crushed by circumstance and weary of their lot had gathered their belongings and set sail for America. The democratic United States had introduced something new onto the world stage, amazing indeed to those who thronged to the sails. They fled toward a country dominated not by kings or queens or nobility but by people like themselves: farmers, planters, carpenters, preachers, candle makers, printers, sailors, and frontiersmen, all determined to live as they, and no one else, saw fit.

It is thanks primarily to the Scottish, Irish, and German immigration into the New World during the eighteenth and nineteenth centuries that so many ancient customs survive. Arriving in America, the immigrants realized that despite crushing prejudice, they could worship or celebrate as they pleased. Memories passed down from days of Celtic or German autonomy stirred into living practice. The old celebrations, long banned in Europe or in the Highlands, or in the valleys of Erse, sparked into life. They live still, during such purely Celtic celebrations as Halloween or feasts deeply influenced by German customs, like the modern Christmas.

A traveler riding through the Shenandoah Valley of Virginia on the last day of October in 1825 would have been startled to see pinpoints of light on every high hill, as if the dark embracing mountains were reflecting the stars. They were bonfires, set by local farmers to celebrate Halloween, the last day of the ancient Celtic year. The traveler surely would have questioned the driver of the coach, who would have explained that the Scottish and Irish settlers in the valley were observing their strange autumn ritual. Had our traveler known the ancient history of the throngs gathered on those chilly, celebratory hills, how astonished he would have been.

Raftery, in his lament, claimed that he, and by implication all of the Irish people, was on a long journey westward. He was referring to Tir Na Nog, the old Irish paradise, which sat far off in the Atlantic Ocean. The Germans, too, had placed their heaven beyond the setting sun. The Greeks knew that the golden apples of immortality lay west of the Pillars of Hercules, and Romans slept outside on summer nights to catch the scent of the western zephyr, fragrant with hope. Now that place, that repository of so much ancient belief, had actually been christened a new country in a new world. America was not a paradise, but in the valleys of the Ohio and the Shenandoah, on the pristine homesteads of Pennsylvania, along the undulating coast of the Chesapeake Bay, the children of Europe had regained the lives of their defeated ancestors.

By the time of Gregory's reform, the year had been divided into eight major turning points. Four of the festivals are, as we have seen, astronomical in origin: the winter and summer solstices and the vernal and autumn equinoxes. These solar signposts told the farmer when to plant and sow, when to reap and store.

In Celtic lands, the old festivals that measured the cattleman's year from the Stone Age to the Industrial Revolution persisted, and, because they split the astronomical quarters, are still called cross-quarter days: November 1, February 1, May 1, and August 1.

Eight days: eight points at which people paused to regard their natural and spiritual progress. Three streams of history had combined to create the Western calendar, the river of time on which we swim.

The first stream bubbled from the low plains of Sumeria and watered the Near East with notions of a predictable universe. It flowed to Greece and finally found its wandering way to Rome, where Caesar commanded the pieties of men to obey the practical dictates of heaven, and created a calendar that finally worked.

Another river now flowed from the north; its rough waters bore pagan mysteries of beast and god, man and woman. This barbarian stream, flowing from Celt and

German, commingled with the Roman during the empire's long rise and slow fall.

The last stream rose again in the east, not far from where the Sumerians first charted out the courses of the sun, moon, and stars. The wastes of Palestine bore a religion that would change not only the face of Europe but the very nature of man. As Europe became Europe, Roman and Celt, Goth and Viking, Greek and Anglo-Saxon, all came to dwell beneath the shadow of the cathedral. That marriage of pagan memory to Christian sensibility produced the feasts of our calendar, which reiterate the histories of their creators.

We will meet those creators again, as we follow the year through its course from New Year's to Christmas. We will walk with Saxons through snow-blanketed forests and hear the hoarse shouts of revelers on the streets of Saturnalia-drunk Rome; meet the druids of Ireland and listen as their descendants rediscover ancient joys in a new land. Our ancestors gave meaning to the passage of time through their reverent imaginations. We can still, if we know how to listen, hear the music they made; music sweet, sad, and strange, still chiming its accompaniment to heaven's perpetual round.

PART TWO

Heaven's Round

Winter

When icicles hang by the wall
And Dick the shepherd blows his nail
And Tom bears logs into the hall,
And milk comes frozen home in pail.
When blood is nipped, and ways be foul,
Then nightly sings the staring owl,
Tu-whit, to-who,
A merry note
While greasy Joan doth stir the pot.
                    —William Shakespeare
                              "Winter"

January

The Father of Morning

Beware the month: bad days
that would take the skin off an ox;
beware of it, and the frosts, which,
as Boreas, the north wind, blow over the land
he gets his breath and rises on the open water
of horse-breeding Thrace and blows,
and the earth and the forest groan
and all the innumerable trees are loud with him.

— Hesiod
Works and Days

n the brittle night sky, the lord of winter reigns, the glittering giant Orion. Astride the celestial equator, and thus seen from every country in the world, Orion is the most well known constellation on earth, his ten bright stars forming the distinct image of a belted warrior. Orion is mentioned in poetry as early as *The Odyssey*; Hesiod, as we have seen, knew him as a harbinger of winter and bad weather. He pursues another winter constellation, the great bull Taurus. In fact an ancient Scottish saying connects Taurus with the new year that January welcomes: "On New Year's Day, the bull rises with the twilight and crosses the sky." The giant chases not just the bull; Greek mythology claims that Orion's real goal sits astride the horns of Taurus, the seven lovely sisters of the Pleiades. Orion's pursuit of Taurus and his heavenly princesses will dominate the canopy of night until spring.

In the northern sky, Ursa Major, the Great Bear, rambles above the pole, followed by her faithful cub Ursa Minor. The Big Dipper, the bear's most famous asterism, stands upright on its handle: a dire scythe poised above the frozen landscape.

January marks the end of the revels that, from the most ancient of days, have celebrated the seeming death and resurrection of the sun at the winter solstice on December 21. December's crowded joys are over: the presents have been opened, the punch drunk to the lees. Carols have been silenced by winter's hush. Time loses its sacred quality and becomes, again, mere time. The child has been born, and it remains to be seen what the world will do with him.

January's reputation, then, is as bleak as its Anglo-Saxon name: Wulfmonath, "month of wolves." The wolves came because they were starving. The cattle they preyed on during the warm months had been safely penned for the winter. Their other staple, the wild deer that still haunt Europe's surviving forests, had either starved, been eaten, or wandered away. Under winter's onslaught, humans retreated into their villages; driven by hunger, the wolves followed. Normally shy of encounters with men, they now appeared in the streets, nipping after the terrified cattle in their pens and snuffling at shuttered windows.

The Saxons were tough, practical people, who gave things names they deserved, and January meant the true beginning of winter: leaves swallowed by snow, days spent trudging through a white landscape on hard errands, and, by the light of the frozen moon, wolves slinking at the edge of town.

January is named after Janus, Roman god of portals and doorways, endings and beginnings. As we have seen, King Numa named the month after popular Janus in an effort to escape godly wrath for adding it to the calendar. A very ancient god even by Roman standards, Janus gave humankind agriculture and law. He sported two heads: one face looked back, into the past; the other forward to the future. Janus occupied the eternal present and served as not only the guardian of time but as the protector of the here and now. His image was placed above doorways, with one face gazing into the house and the other out into the world.

Janus, god of portals and doorways, endings and beginnings.

As the god of time, Janus presided over all moments of transition: dawn, noon, dusk, midnight. The Romans also called him, with deep filial affection, Pater Matuninus, the Father of Morning, because Janus rolled back the night and woke the sun. In keeping with his dual nature, Janus also brought on the shades of night. He guarded thresholds, crossroads, shipyards, graves. He was the first god the Romans prayed to in the morning and last god they prayed to before they went to bed. Unlike our God, who stands outside of time and looks at us, Janus was time, and the month named after him, the gateway of the year, partook of his dual nature.

January is still a month of dualities and contradictions. Although it is thought of as the opening of gloomy winter after the lights and joys of the holidays, January is also one of the most beautiful months of the year. Nature reveals herself without artifice. Sunlight falls on bare branch, on stone or earth, revealing the hidden contours of nature, the simple skeleton of creation. Birdsong is more thrilling for being rare, and each creature glimpsed on a long woodland walk seems like a surviving gift. January bears a vast silence that teaches us to wait for a moment between what came before, and what will follow after.

January 1

New Year's Day

Ring out, wild bells, to the wild wild night,
The year is dying in the night.

— Alfred, Lord Tennyson

Throughout history, civilizations have chosen a wide range of days on which to celebrate the New Year. The Egyptians and Persians observed New Year's on the vernal equinox; the early Athenians chose the winter solstice, and then switched their new year under Pericles to June 21, the summer solstice. In Rome, which had used a wide variety of dates over the centuries, Caesar officially proclaimed January 1 as New Year's Day. The Romans proceeded to ignore him.

In Europe, after the conversion, New Year's was widely celebrated on March 25. This is because the ecclesiastical year begins at the vernal equinox, and pious Christians throughout Europe naturally began to hold their New Year's observances to coincide with the church calendar. The rivalry between January 1 and March 25 continued throughout the Middle Ages; not until the

Gregorian reforms was the former date widely and finally accepted by most nations. England, however, held on to the old March date until 1753, as did its colonies.

The Romans celebrated the winter solstice with a citywide orgy called the Saturnalia, which we will visit at the end of the year. In short, they celebrated the good old days of Saturn's reign, when men were happier and the world more full of delights. At the close of Saturn's reign (he was overthrown by Jupiter), this onetime father of the gods retreated beyond the horizon, despondent and alone. His planet, which often rose in the winter months, was said to infect men with dolorous thoughts. During the Saturnalia, the Romans threw one last bash in Saturn's name, reliving the good old days, before the onset of the terrible winter months. After the reformation of the calendar, the Romans used the new January 1 date as an excuse to continue their Saturnalia into the New Year, and developed customs that still survive. The poet Ovid describes some of them: all "work, litigation and strife" was suspended across the empire; estranged friends were reconciled; white-robed priests led vast processions of the hopeful to the Capitol for sacrifices to Janus.

Romans held open houses, inviting friends and relations to stop by for a bite to eat and a few glasses of wine. They held elaborate masques, during which costumed Romans danced, sang, and drank. During these visits, small presents, called *strenae*, were exchanged. As Rome grew wealthier, these parties grew absurdly extravagant, and the Romans consumed herds of oxen and vineyards of wine in the name of a good time.

The Romans were not alone in partying at this time of year; among the ancient Teutons, the period around the winter solstice was also a time of drunken celebration. By the fifth century, as we shall see, the primary celebrations of the season had been fixed on December 25, Christmas Day, and January 1 had assumed a serious, sacred character as the Feast of the Circumcision. The church tried to combat the old propensity for merrymaking on this day, as canon 17 of the Council of Tours (567) makes plain: "In order to tread under foot the customs of the heathen, our fathers ordain that private litanies should be held at the beginning of January, psalms sung in churches, and the mass of circumcision, pleasing to God."

None of the church's edicts did much good to quell the festivities. Rather than restricting merrymaking to one day amid the season, the close proximity of Christmas and New Year's gave people an excuse to overindulge from mid-December to early January. This twelve-day period of license is still with us.

In Celtic countries like Scotland and Ireland, many of the customs that had been celebrated during the ancient New Year's festival of Samhain (see Halloween) were transferred to January 1. The old year was "burned out" by bonfires lit on hilltops and in village squares; children went about in old-time costumes begging for treats; fortune-telling and thoughts of the dead abounded.

The celebratory period ends with Epiphany. In the Greek, the word *epiphaneiae* means "appearance" or "manifestation"; it commemorates the arrival of the Kings (or wise men) of the East to the manger in Bethlehem, where the Christ child lay swaddled in a manger. The first Monday after the Epiphany is called Plough Day in England, and a drear day it is, when men and women who have luxuriated in the delights of the Yuletide must set themselves back to work, or "behind the plough." January now reigns, hard work and short days, phlegmatic as old exiled Saturn.

The father of the New Year, Janus, is with us still, in a way. In fact, some of his ancient followers can be seen on magazine covers during the first week of January. How they got from Rome to Madison Avenue is a complicated story, but not terribly hard to follow.

Janus probably had worshippers in Italy long before the Romans emerged. In fact, he was only one of many sky gods worshipped throughout the ancient world, all related to the great sky god of the Indo-Europeans, a still-mysterious people who spread from their original homeland in the Ural Mountains before recorded history to influence civilizations from China to Ireland.

The original name of the seminal Indo-European

god was cognitive with their word for light, *diovis.* The Greeks turned this word into Zeus, their chief deity. The Romans renamed Zeus Zeus Pater, Zeus the Father. Zeus Pater, with casual usage, became Deuspater: speak the name quickly and you'll see how easily the god became known by classical times as Jupiter. Jupiter replaced Janus as the chief god of the Roman pantheon, and in so doing borrowed many of the older fellow's attributes, including the habit of speaking through the sacred oak.

Worship of the oak was common throughout ancient Europe. When the Romans conquered the Celtic world and encountered the druids, they were shocked to learn that these primitive wizards shared with sophisticated Roman augurs a sublime reverence for the oak tree. On the oaks of northern Europe grew a parasitic plant that kept its green leaves throughout the winter. Because this plant grew on the sacred oak, and bloomed even during the coldest days of winter, it came to be seen as sacred in itself.

We know it as the mistletoe, symbol of life in winter's darkness; as we shall see later, it still adorns thresholds at Christmas. In Celtic Europe, druid priests clambered up their sacred oaks and, using golden sickles, collected the mistletoe for use in magical rites. Even after the Romans suppressed the druidic cults, the common people continued to collect mistletoe during the winter; and the memory of the wise old druids gathering their precious mistletoe by moonlight never left the folk consciousness of northern Europeans. When the great Irish and Scottish immigrations into North America began during the nineteenth century, the people brought their folk beliefs with them.

And so, after a long road, we return finally to a still-surviving symbol of New Year's, that hinge day of all the year, the door through which we all pass as we move from the past into the future: an old man in a flowing robe, hoisting over his shoulder a scythe. Many think of him as Father Time, but look in his pockets: you're sure to find a clump of mistletoe there.

Our druid brings an ancient message. Although the Yuletide revels are over, the result of their magic is not. The sun climbs higher with each passing day; the holy child grows stronger. He reminds us that January is the portal of the year, opening onto a present in which the world, reborn at the turning of the sun, begins to re-create itself. In spite of its darkness, January, like its god, is the father of the year's morning.

Druid.

February

The Secret Birth

Lenten is come with love to toune
With blossom and with brides run
That all this blessing bringeth
Days-eyes in the dales
Notes suete of nytengales
Uch foul song singeth

— Anonymous,
thirteenth century

lthough mighty Orion still commands the southern sky, Leo, who now springs in from the north, threatens his reign; below Leo's haunches, gentle Virgo peeps above the eastern horizon. Directly overhead stand Castor and Pollux, the Gemini twins. These sons of beautiful Leda, whom Zeus ravaged in the form of a swan, were thought by the ancients to stand guard over mortal adventurers during this cold and dangerous time of the year. Greek sailors looked up to them for protection as they fought the choppy waves, and Roman cavalrymen often finished oaths by swearing, "by Gemini," which American sailors later turned into "by Jimminy." The valiant brothers see their charges through to another spring.

As we've seen, February was the month of purification among the ancient Romans: *februo*, "I purify by sacrifice." Remember that this was the terror time of the year: even in the later days of the republic, the Romans held their great supernatural festivals during February, which hearkened back to the days when the month was given wholly to the worship of the deities of the underworld.

The Anglo-Saxons called February several names: "Sprout-kale," from the sprouting of cabbage or kale, and "Fill-dike," when the rain and melting snow fills the ditches to overflowing:

> February be Fill-dike,
> be it black or be it white,
> But if it be white
> it's the better to like.

Thanks to the church, the Anglo-Saxons took up some of the old Roman notions and observed February as a month of sacrifice and negation. In the few remaining Celtic countries like Ireland, it marked the end of winter, and was observed as a time of hope and renewal, a promise of a promise of spring.

February is a womb, rich with the hidden promises of the frozen earth. Although winter's grip still clutches the world, small signs of rebirth are everywhere. Each day, the sun climbs higher in the sky, the days grow perceptibly longer, and, deep in the secret places of the earth, ice thaws, bulbs crack, shoots creep toward the crust. The feasts of February are predictive, describing not only the still-wintry condition of the earth but also the imminent approach of spring. Just as the pregnancy of ewes and the slow rekindling of the warmth of the sun point toward warmer days, so too do the sere days of Lenten abstinence, inaugurated in February, promise the eventual triumph of the risen Christ at Eastertide.

February 1 and 2

Cross-Quarter Day

Imbolc, Candlemas, and Groundhog Day

People come — they stay for a while, they flourish, they build — and they go. It is their way. But we remain. There were badgers here, I've been told, long before that same city ever came to be. And now there are badgers here again. We are an enduring lot, and we may move out for a time, but we wait, and are patient, and back we come. And so it will ever be.

— Kenneth Grahame
The Wind in the Willows

And so it remains of this feast: long forgotten, transformed, and, because it is a secret sharing, immortal. Larger feasts have obscured it, and what began as a sacred rite in ancient days is now filler for the ten o'clock news. But the earth remembers, and so do the badgers.

An old European folk belief predicts that if the weather is fine and frosty at the beginning of February, there is more winter ahead than behind. Another claims that if the dikes are full of water at the first of the month, winter will not last much longer. The first of the month is a time for augury, a time to wait with the hushed world to see if the distant spring will favor the farmer with an early arrival.

This could mean the difference between life and death, poverty or plenty. At about this time of year, on homesteads throughout Europe, pregnant sheep begin to lactate in preparation for the birth of their lambs in March. If the weather in February is kind, they stand a good chance of delivering their lambs safely, and the lambs stand a better chance of surviving. Over the centuries, anxious husbandmen throughout Europe have tried to prompt winter into an early exit.

The ancient Irish did one better: they summoned the goddess of fire on February 1 to chase winter away. Her name was Brigit (sometimes spelled Brigid), and she was possibly the most beloved of the Celts' many goddesses. As the mistress of fertility, she blessed humans and animals alike. Women prayed to her when they wished to become pregnant, and afterward for a safe delivery. As goddess of all household arts, she aided young mothers in raising their children, and inspired poetry — indispensable for a happy household — in a few chosen souls.

The last day of January was known by the old Celtic calendar as Brigit's Night, and divided the winter from the spring. This was also the final night of the reign of the Cailleac, the hag. The loathly lady was hideous and ancient, but also dreadfully wise. She lived in mountain cairns amid the lonely creatures of the hills, and those who sought wisdom at her feet either returned enlightened or did not return at all. Her ugliness, age, and wisdom reflected the severe, contemplative days of winter.

This is a terribly important figure, this Cailleac. She dwelt, and still dwells, in the depths of human imagination. A font of wisdom, she is as lethal as a rattler; if you bow before her as a fool, her poisonous wisdom will strike you dead to the ground. She keeps company with the oracular priestess of the famous temple of Delphi in Greece and the sacred whore of the Ziggurat in Babylon. A nasty character, dangerous and vital to know, she will fill your head with wisdom or your heart with fatal spleen. We will meet her again.

February 1, called Imbolc, inaugurated Brigit's reign. The ewes, now come into their milk, were driven through hoops of flame to receive the purification and protection of the goddess.

Brigit was so important to the Irish that when the Catholic Church arrived, they made a saint of her; one of the patron saints of Ireland, in fact. Most of the old goddess's attributes were smoothly transferred to the saint: her feast day still falls on Imbolc, and, like her divine namesake, she watches over mothers, cattle, and poets. And she still tended her sacred fire; the saint's legend claims that at her nunnery in Kildare, she and nineteen nuns watched over an eternal flame. The nuns of Kildare in fact, tended a fire there until the late Middle Ages.

This passage from the medieval *Book of Lismore* lets us observe the process, seamless and poetic, by which the Irish converted their ancient gods to the service of Christ:

> It is she Brigid that helpeth everyone who is in danger: it is she that abaiteth the pestilences; it is she that quelleth the rage and the storm of the sea. She is the profettes of the Christ; she is the queen of the south; she is the Mary of the Gael.

Fires also flickered on the streets of Rome three thousand years ago. During the opening days of dreadful February, the ancient Romans had a custom of carrying burning candles through the streets and fields to frighten away the evil spirits that clustered in the air. The Christian church adopted the festival as their own around the year 600, an appropriation freely admitted later by Pope Innocent the XII, during a sermon:

> Why do we in this feast carry candles? Because the Gentiles (i.e., pagans) dedicated the month of February to the infernal gods . . . and as at the beginning of it

Pluto stole Persephone, and her mother Ceres sought her in the night with lighted candles, so they, at the beginning of this month, walked about the city with lighted candles. Because the holy fathers could not extirpate this custom, they ordained that Christians should carry about candles in honor of the Blessed Virgin; and thus what was done before to the honor of Ceres is now done for the honor of the Virgin.

And so it was: Candlemas was for centuries the Feast of the Purification of the Virgin Mary. Although it is now called the Purification of the Lord, February 2 is still sacred to fire. On that day, in Roman Catholic and Greek churches throughout the world, all of the candles that will be used during services throughout the year are consecrated. The priest then distributes some of them to the congregation, who form a processional from the sanctuary and into the streets.

In Europe, although the old Roman and Celtic fire festivals became Christianized, the idea of February 1 as a harbinger of spring lingered on. Many prognosticating superstitions clustered around the opening of February, and were captured in an old German rhyme:

> If Candlemas Day be dry and fair,
> The half o'winter's to come in mair [March]
> If Candlemas Day be wet and foul,
> The half o' winter's gane at Yule.

In a sort of reverse magic, it was assumed that a bright and mild opening to February promised bad weather ahead, and six more weeks of winter; a gray and chilly day meant that spring would arrive early.

Enter now the badger. If spring was already brewing under the surface of the earth, then the badger, who slept amid the roots and tubers, could be expected to give a report on the condition of things down there. Over the years, Saxons and Germans developed the notion that if the badger saw his shadow at the opening of February, winter would linger on. This belief became so widespread throughout the northern countries that when German immigrants settled in America, they brought the tradition with them. The New World, however, had new animals, and the old powers of the badger were transferred to the American groundhog. Another servant of Brigit has appeared, and we can be sure that the dear old saint, formerly goddess, has added him to her litany of beloved and protected creatures.

February 15

The Lupercal, Saint Valentine's Day

Oft have I heard both youth and virgin say
Birds choose their mates and couples too this day
But by their flight I never can divine
When I shall couple with my Valentine.

> — Robert Herrick
> "Valentines"

These two celebrations reveal a hidden stream of ritual. The Romans celebrated the Lupercal as a combination of horror show and fertility rite. How this primitive, violent feast became a celebration of a Catholic saint, and, even odder, how the pious church came to lend the name of a celibate martyr to a feast for lovers, is an odd story, involving everything from werewolves to track and field. And lots of blood.

Atavistic and weird, the Lupercal, which means "wolf day," rises like an ancient stone totem from the manicured Roman calendar. It was held in honor of Lupercus, the Roman equivalent of the Greek nature god

Pan, so called because he protected the flocks from wolves. The Lupercal was one of the most ancient of Roman festivals, predating even the founding of the city. Like the Celtic Imbolc, the Lupercal was a festival of expiation and purification, meant to bring fertility to the community. In early times humans were sacrificed after being driven around the walls of the city; later, the victims became a goat and a dog, both symbols of procreation. After being slaughtered, their blood was smeared on the foreheads of two youths, and then wiped off with wool moistened with ewe's milk.

After the feast, the celebrants, naked except for a goatskin apron, ran around the old line of the Palatine walls, striking all whom they met with thongs made from the skins of the slaughtered animals. These blows were reputed to endow women with fertility. Afterward, Roman citizens of every class stripped naked and copulated in the streets. The Lupercal marked a true return to primitivism: a festival of death, fertility, blood, and sex.

It remains so today, albeit in a bowdlerized, sanitized form, thanks to two martyrs named Valentine. Although they are almost certainly derived from one individual, tradition states that both of these brave men lived around A.D. 270. The first Valentine was a priest of the Roman state religion who was imprisoned for harboring Christians. While awaiting sentence, he cured the jailer's daughter of her blindness and was rewarded for his miraculous leechcraft by being beaten to death with clubs. The other was a bishop of Terni who met a similar unpleasant fate in Rome.

How did two celibate martyrs become the patron saints of lovers? One tradition, mentioned by Chaucer, holds that birds begin seeking their mates around February 14, and that because of this Saint Valentine became the natural patron of all lovers. More likely, the blood and passion of the Lupercal, long remembered by the Italian descendants of Rome, transformed the blood of the slaughtered saints into the bright red hearts of Valentine's Day. And Valentine's colors have never changed. The windows of grade schools are peppered with pasted hearts: smatterings of red on a frosted pane, like the flecks of blood flayed from the backs of Roman women, scourged into fecundity; like the flecks of Valentine's blood peppering his chaste cell.

Lent

Tis a fast to dole
Thy sheaf of wheat,
And meat,
Unto the hungry soul.
It is to fast from strife,
From old debate
And hate;
To circumcise thy life
To show a heart grief-rent
To starve thy sin,
Not bin;
And that's to keep thy Lent.

— Robert Herrick
"Noble Numbers"

hristianity transformed old customs of purification and fertility into an organized period of penance and self-negation. Pagan observances like Imbolc and the Lupercal served to purify the young within their mothers' wombs as a prelude to birth;

Lent sanctifies not the ripening womb, but the ripening soul.

Beginning on Ash Wednesday, Lent lasts for forty days, in imitation of Christ's self-imposed exile in the desert at the beginning of his mission. During this time, the faithful are expected to give up vices or pleasurable habits, pray and attend mass more frequently, and meditate on the state of their souls. In medieval times, people donned sackcloth, smeared their faces with ash and water, flogged themselves, and forswore most food and drink during the Lenten observance. In spite of its severe customs, Lent is a hopeful time. The word comes from the Middle English word *lengten*, or "lengthen": a reference to the fact that the days mercifully grow longer during this time.

Of course, people being people, all of this Lenten self-sacrifice had to be rewarded before it even began. Throughout Europe, for three days before the beginning of Lent, businesses closed, streets were blocked off, and everyone headed for church, where they went to confession. Afterward, kegs were tapped, bottles drained, and sweetmeats and other foods soon to be forbidden were consumed in a bout of wild merrymaking.

Eventually these pre-Lenten revels became concentrated into the Tuesday before Ash Wednesday, called Pancake Day after the sweet pancakes traditionally eaten during the party. In medieval France, where the day was known as *mardi gras*, or Fat Tuesday, a vast carnival was celebrated, during which an enormous ox was paraded through the streets of Paris, surrounded by common folk dressed blasphemously as priests and nuns. The people banged drums and kettles in an unconscious imitation of a Roman triumphal parade. Years later, in France's former, debauched colony of New Orleans, the party known as Mardi Gras became America's most famous orgy, and a raucous song in the depths of winter. Eventually, however, in New Orleans as in all Christian lands, Lent arrives with the gray dawn of Ash Wednesday.

Ash Wednesday, calculated backward forty days from the date of Easter, always falls in February. It is so-named because on that day Catholics stand before the church altar and receive on their foreheads a smeared cross of ash from the priest, along with an admonition that, in some churches, is still whispered in Latin:

> Memento, homo, quia ceneris est,
> Et in cenerum revertasis.

> [Remember, man, that thou art dust,
> and unto dust thou shalt return.]

The ashes come from a very specific source. On Palm Sunday, one week before Easter, members of the congregation hold palm fronds, in imitation of the crowds who welcomed Christ into Jerusalem. Afterward, the palms are ceremoniously burned, their ashes collected and stored. They reappear the following year, on Ash Wednesday, to be daubed on the foreheads of the faithful. The symbolism of Ash Wednesday's ashes is circular, striking, and sublime. A year after the savior's symbolic entrance into the city, the very ashes of the banners once held forth to honor him now prepare the faithful for the season of his crucifixion.

Some things, some impulses, cannot be masked, even by new gods. The immolated god is smeared to the face, just as wailing Romans three thousand years ago fingered the symbolic ashes of their ancestors and contemplated their own final fate. In February, holocausts lit three millennia ago still burn.

March

Rain, Mud, and Hope

Oh Westron Wind when wilt thou blow?
The small rains down can rain.
Christ that my love were in my arms
And I in my bed again.

— Anonymous,
twelfth century

 arch begins with the blare of heaven's trumpets. Wind, stirred into life by the radiant warmth of the young sun, lashes the budding trees. As if in keeping with March's martial airs, the night sky announces Auriga, the charioteer. Auriga clatters across the northern skies behind a team of goats led by Capella, a bright star thought by the Greeks to be Amalthea, the young she-goat who suckled Zeus as a baby. Young Zeus, unaware of his strength, reached out to grasp Amalthea's horn and snapped it off. As reparation, he transformed her lost horn into a magical, endless source of food and drink: the cornucopia.

The month's old Saxon name was Hrethmonath, "rough month," after the boisterous winds; the Dutch called it Lentmaand, "the time of Lent." In more ancient days, March's winds competed with the bray of martial trumpets; it signaled the start of Roman military operations after a winter hiatus and still bears the name of their god of war, mighty, merciless Mars.

Roman tradition held that Mars was the father of Romulus, and actually instructed him in the creation of the first Roman calendar. Romulus then honored his father by making his month the first of the year. Since the Romans prided themselves on being a nation of sturdy farmers, Mars was also the patron saint of those who tilled the land.

The month and all born in it belonged to that terrible god, whose blood-red planet was said to drive men to carnage. The *Compost of Ptholomeus*, an almanac from the Middle Ages, claims that unto Mars

> is borne thieves and robbers, nyght walkers and quarell pykers, bosters, mockers, and skoffers; and these men of Mars causeth war, and murther, and batayle. They will be gladly smythes or workers of iryon, lyers, great swearers.

For a long time, as we have seen, the Romans celebrated their new year not on the first of January but in

March. Spring had come, and the sere days of winter were already fading into memory. During March the lambs arrived, quivering with hope, and the planting that would bring the next year's harvest was cast into the fields. The arrival of March was good news.

The murder of Julius Caesar changed all that, and gave March a bloody hue. After the assassination, its ides, the fifteenth, became — and, thanks largely to William Shakespeare, remains — an uneasy watchword for imminent disaster.

March is a time of delayed pleasure. Spring still dances over the distant hills, taunting those who have kept faith in spite of all appearances. The month opens in wintry Lenten gloom, but soon seems to soften toward Easter. River ice melts, and robins return. The whispered promise of the sun at winter solstice takes full voice as the creeks slowly thaw and the hard loam melts into butter. Then, suddenly, a bitter wind kills early buds, and the lakes, which seemed only days away from welcoming swimmers, harden with new ice. March tests our faith. It can summon all the bluster of its namesake to convince huddled mortals that the power of winter, like that of any tyrant, is not soon or lightly surrendered. On a night in late March the wind can blow with a force unfelt all winter. Fear not. Beneath the angry skies, fragile as parchment but as irresistible as time, crocuses push their shafts up through the damp earth.

March 20–25

Quarter Day

The Vernal Equinox, Lady Day, Old New Year's

The old Roman year began in March, with the Roman New Year falling on or near the vernal equinox, until Caesar's stringent reforms transferred it to January. The Romans had inherited their New Year's festival from other, older cultures. Throughout the ancient world, in fact, New Year's Day was logically celebrated in the spring, when the world indeed seemed new. On the vernal equinox, after months of long nights and short days, day and night lasted an equal amount of time. People knew that the cosmic balance would now swing in favor of the sun.

After Caesar, Roman calendars continued to mark January 1 as the date of the New Year. Not even great Caesar's ghost, however, could control the common people's will toward their own custom. Romans of city and country continued to celebrate the New Year with the coming of spring, when nature told them more accurately than any calendar that the world was returning to life. This custom survived well into medieval Christian Europe, and didn't really peter out until the Gregorian calendar reforms of the sixteenth century. Even then, because of the Protestant resistance against the pope's reform, the first of March was observed as New Year's Day in England and Scotland well into the eighteenth century.

Lady Day, on March 25, commemorates the Annunciation of the Virgin Mary, when the angel Gabriel brought Mary the news that she carried within her womb the son of God. For years it was called Saint Mary's Day in Lent, to distinguish it from the myriad festivals in honor of the Virgin that peppered the medieval calendar. Lady Day assumed many of the qualities of the old New Year's festivals, and was spared by custom — if not by church sanction — from the strict daily observances of Lent. People could dance, drink, and gorge at communal tables throughout the land.

Many Christian cultures still celebrate some form of break from Lenten strictures around the vernal equinox. The most famous of these festivals to survive is the celebration of Saint Patrick's Day, when Irish throughout the world (and especially in the United States) relax from both Lent and winter to celebrate their common heritage with cheerful drink and music. March 17, the saint's great day, may be bitterly cold, with the wind howling and sleet blowing outside the pub's window, but to Irish all over the world, it means, beyond the revelry, one thing: Spring's around the bend.

Spring

I wandered lonely as a cloud
That floats on high o'er vales and hills,
When all at once I saw a crowd,
A host, of golden daffodils;
Beside the lake, beneath the trees,
Fluttering and dancing in the breeze.
— William Wordsworth
"The Daffodils"

April

Awake!

Whan that April with his showers soote
The drought of March hath perced to the roote
And bathed every veyne in swich licour
Of which virtu engendered is the flour . . .

— Geoffrey Chaucer
The Canterbury Tales

pril's nights are filled with falling blossom. High above, Vega, the earliest of the great summer stars, rises in the northeast. Shining blue-white, like a rare celestial diamond, Vega forms the centerpiece of Lyra, the lyre of Orpheus.

The finest singer in the world, Orpheus could charm the very rocks and stones to weep. When his young lover Eurydice suddenly died, Orpheus journeyed alone to the underworld and, through his plaintive lament for his dead love, won the pity of even pitiless Hades, the god of the dead. Eurydice, Hades decreed, could follow Orpheus back to the living world — but on one condition: Orpheus could not look back until he had reached the sunlight. The singer agreed. He set out, climbing up through the long black tunnel out of hell. At the final moment, before the final shadows parted, torn by anxiety, Orpheus looked back. The last sight he had of Eurydice was of a weeping, retreating ghost. He met his own end shortly afterward, torn to bits by wild maenads whom he, in his grief, could not appease with his gentle song. Zeus, who understood what the world had lost, hung the lyre of Orpheus in the sky, where it shines again during the first weeks of April, an emblem of this month so kind and cruel to lovers.

April derives from the Latin word *aperire*, literally, "to open." Now nature wakes from her winter sleep and opens her womb to deliver new life. Hearts open as well. There are certain mornings in April — clear, crisp, with a faint scent of wet life on the cool breeze and birdsong rising in the pale green of the willows — that surely carry some memory of the first fine mornings of the world.

Spring's messengers arrive on wings to announce her return. In Europe, the cry of the cuckoo still calls people to set their tasks aside for a while and listen to the messenger of spring.[8] In America, spotting the first cheerful robin is a necessary ritual of the season.

The season brings forth flowers, which may bring forth thorns. April is the month of love: love of the world's exquisite beauties, and of a man for a woman, love found, or sometimes only grasped and lost, during this delicate time of beauty and regeneration. The transience of life's passion is felt most keenly not during gray winter but in April, when the earth returns from the underworld, singing the song of heartbroken Orpheus.

---

[8]Some time ago I was visiting a small fishing village in Ireland at the end of April. Every evening, the owner of the village pub, a grand and patient lady, stepped out from behind the bar, clambered onto her bicycle, and pedaled away into the dusk. She was off to a small thicket at the edge of town, where, local rumor claimed, a cuckoo was nesting. After several evenings of trying, she heard the bird sing and returned to her patrons with glad eyes.

April 1

April Fool's Day

A very strange day, on which practical jokes prevail. These usually take the form of false alarms, but traditionally an "April Fool" involves sending some poor dupe out on a fruitless or nonexistent errand. The day's origins are very obscure and still hotly debated by folklorists. Some claim that April Fool's is of extreme antiquity, and probably began as the final day of the weeklong observances of the vernal equinox celebrated widely by Indo-European people throughout the ancient world. Others place its origin at a far later time, perhaps as late as the sixteenth century. The theories are many, fascinating, and contradictory.

Here are a few: that the day's false errands duplicate the fruitless mission of the dove sent out of the ark by Noah; that they imitate Christ's wanderings from Pilate to King Herod and back on the eve of his crucifixion; that the Romans actually began the pranks during their feast of Aprilis, a giddy festival celebrating the first plantings of the season, when the farmers cast cares aside as they cast their seeds; or simply that early spring's uncertain weather, which fools everybody on a daily basis, proved the model for the misbehavior.

William Walsh, in his odd and lively compendium of folklore, *Curiosities of Popular Customs* (1893), places the origins of April Fool's in the East, and goes on to make a bizarre argument linking it with the Gregorian reforms:

> The proof of the great antiquity of the observance of this festival, as well as the probability of its original establishment in an Asiatic region, arises from the evidence of facts afforded us by astronomy. As we have seen, the long struggle between January and March over which month should herald the New Year ended with the Gregorian reforms. In Asia, a similar change occurred, as the shifting of the equinoctial points, caused by the precession of the equinoxes, changed the astronomical calculation of New Years.

An article in a 1766 issue of the *Gentleman's Magazine* of London seems to lay the origin squarely on Gregory's papal shoulders. Since for hundreds of years New Year's Day fell on the twenty-fifth of March, April 1 would have been the concluding day of the weeklong festivities. After the reform, those backward souls who still celebrated the New Year on April 1 were labeled April Fools by their more knowledgeable countrymen, and became the butts of all sorts of jokes.

Proof that April Fool's really is an ancient remnant of some long-forgotten Indo-European rite comes from India, where the last week of March is still celebrated as the Huli, a time of merriment and tricks; a favorite Huli prank is to send people on useless or foolish errands.

In Europe (a friend tells me that Italy is infected with the practice), England, and America, the custom of April fooling continues to this day. In Scotland, the victim of an April Fool's prank is called the April Gawk, *gawk* being a derivation of the old Teutonic word *gauch*, meaning "cuckoo." The cuckoo, which lays her eggs in other birds' nests, leaving the hard work of rearing her chicks to others, serves as a natural model for tricksters.

In keeping with the spirit of the day, let us accept all the above explanations as little more than fool's errands, and enjoy this silly day for what it is — a gasp of nonsensical delight at the dawn of spring.

Passover, Easter

The Dancing Sun

Dance, dance, wherever you may be
I am the Lord of the Dance said he
And I'll lead you on, whoever you may be,
For I am the Lord of the Dance said he.

> — Anonymous
> "Lord of the Dance"

 aster is the most important feast of the Christian year. It falls on the Sunday after the first full moon following the vernal equinox, an arcane bit of measurement that derives from the Jewish religious calendar. Christ's crucifixion coincided with the Jewish Passover, which was always celebrated on the fourteenth or fifteenth day of Nissan, a month corresponding with April. Since Jewish months always begin at the rising of the new moon, the middle of the month always falls after the full moon has risen.

The great Hebrew feast of Passover always occurred

during this time. It reiterated two very sacred moments: the coming of spring, as symbolized by the slaughter of the first lambs during the bracing early days of the season (in keeping this feast, the Hebrews were in line with virtually every other ancient society), and, more crucially, the deliverance of the Jews from out of bondage in Egypt by their deliverer Moses, during the Exodus.

The tale of the Exodus is known throughout the world. Moses was born a Hebrew. His mother, to avoid his slaughter at the hands of Egyptian soldiers who had been ordered to kill all firstborn Hebrew children, sent the infant Moses down the Nile in a basket of reeds. Pharaoh's wife found him there amid the reeds and raised him as a privileged member of the royal family. Moses' life changed when he saw an Egyptian brutally beat a Hebrew. In a fury, he killed the Egyptian and fled into the Midian desert, where he lived with the shepherds and took a wife. He also spent time amid the wastes, roaming the sere mountains and the alkaloid valleys, searching for the truth of his life.

He found it. On a pilgrimage into the mountains, he encountered the burning bush.

The rest is as known as spring itself. Moses returned to Egypt, now as the prophet of Yahweh. He demanded that pharaoh (by tradition Ramses) let his people go. Pharaoh balked, willfully. Seven plagues followed, the last of which was the most terrible. In a repetition of the threat that had endangered Moses' own young life, Yahweh inspired Moses to inform the pharaoh that, if the Hebrew nation was not released, the firstborn of every Egyptian would be taken on the night of the Hebrew festival of Passover. To protect the Hebrews from God's messenger, the angel of death, Moses told his people to follow the ancient customs of the evening — most especially to smear the blood of the slaughtered lamb on their doors. Thus the angel would pass over.

The angels passed over the Hebrews' houses, while the Egyptian fathers and mothers screamed in terror as their children died. After the long night of terror, the Hebrews were released by the pharaoh (he tried one more time to enslave them again, with disastrous results involving the Red Sea).

Every year, ever after, the Hebrews of their struggling nation gathered to celebrate both the old spring festival and their great liberation. They ate bitter herbs at the seder meal, like garlic and hyssop; baked unleavened bread in their ovens to symbolize the bread their forebears did not have time to let rise before they fled, a bread of freedom and affliction; and drank sweet wine, delivered by God, to remind them that his long promise had been redeemed.

Early Christian leaders wanted to keep the observance of Christ's death and resurrection connected to the Passover for symbolic reasons — he was the Paschal

Lamb of mankind, the great sacrifice that fulfilled the promises of the prophets — so they tagged the observance of Easter onto the calculation of the Passover rite.

An older custom also connects Christ with the vernal equinox. Semitic mythologies all featured gods who died, often violently, to ensure the fecundity of the earth. The Egyptians worshipped Osiris, god of agriculture, death, and resurrection, who had been killed by his jealous brother Set only to be revived by his wife, Isis. The Egyptians reenacted the Osiris story every year in fertility dramas that coincided with the flooding of the Nile, the start of the spring planting season.

The Greeks worshipped Adonis, their version of the Middle Eastern fertility god Tammus. The cult of Adonis moved from Babylonia into mainland Greece, where it flourished. The Adonis story follows the same pattern as that of Osiris. While hunting, Adonis slew a dangerous boar but was killed in the act; at the spot, the red anemone flower sprang up, stained by Adonis's blood. Aphrodite, the goddess of love and Adonis's lover, wandered the earth for some sign of him; while she did, no passion stirred in the breasts of men and women, no crops or flowers grew, and earth became as barren and cold as a spurned lover. Eventually Zeus allowed Adonis to be reborn each spring and spend half the year with Aphrodite.

Every year, in the early spring, the followers of Adonis would gather together to mourn his death. They cast wooden carvings of the god into the sea and sang a hymn of hope for his return. They also prepared baskets containing an image of Adonis and an assortment of flowers, called "little gardens of Adonis," which they would float out into the river until the current carried them away. Seven days later, when the red anemone bloomed in the woodlands, the faithful would rejoice at the resurrection of their god and the earth.

These rites and ceremonies will sound familiar to anyone who has attended a sunrise mass on Easter morning or prepared an Easter basket. Like Osiris and Adonis, Christ is a sacrificial god whose death ensures the rebirth of the world. The vast difference between Christ and his predecessors lies in the fact that Osiris and Adonis perished to ensure the sexual fecundity of creation, while Christ's sacrifice was interpreted as cleansing the spiritual pollution of the Fall; this, in a nutshell, demonstrates the difference in attitudes toward divinity between the pagan world and the Christian that conquered it.

The Venerable Bede, in his *History of the Anglo-Saxons*, derives the word *Easter* from the Saxon goddess Eostre, and this etymology has held up over the years. Eostre was the goddess of the spring, and her consort was none other than the hare, a figure who still appears at Easter. Now called the Easter Bunny, he brings with him the oldest symbol of the season, the egg.

Eggs are universal symbols of life and the cosmos, and the custom of giving them away, hiding them, decorating them, and eating them at the time of the vernal equinox is as ancient as it is widespread. Egyptians boiled eggs in remembrance of humanity's survival of the devastating primordial flood that features so largely in Semitic mythologies from Gilgamesh to Noah. Jews ate them with the Passover lamb in celebration of their successful flight from Egypt.

Christians considered the egg, seemingly inert but hiding inner life, a potent symbol of the Resurrection. They decorated their Easter eggs, in the words of folk-lore scholar William Walsh, "as a religious trophy after Lent's last days of penitence and mortification, as a totem of simple celebration; also, more profoundly, as an emblem of the resurrection of the Christ from the regions of death and the grave."

Easter's advent carries none of the breathless anticipation of Christmas, but its joys are deeper and more lasting. The fasts of Lent are over, the earth has come back to life, and, for believers, the Savior is stirring in his grave, soon to reappear on the face of the earth in shining glory. On the dawn of Easter Sunday, church bells ring, choruses raise their voices to the young sun, new candles are carried into darkened churches, and the Lenten purple is torn from the altar, replaced by the flowers of spring.

The Celtic peoples, poetic as usual, claim that the rising sun actually dances on Easter morning, and to this day people in Ireland, Scotland, and parts of England get up before dawn and head for the nearest hilltop.

May

The Piper at the Gates of Dawn

Sudden and magnificent, the sun's broad golden disk showed itself over the horizon facing them; and the first rays, shooting across the level water-meadows, took the animals full in the eyes and dazzled them. When they were able to look once more, the vision had vanished, and the air was full of the carol of birds that had hailed the dawn.

— Kenneth Grahame
The Wind in the Willows

he Big Dipper tilts against the night sky, an emptying ladle that showers the heavens with stars. Blue Vega rises higher with each passing evening, carrying summer aloft. Below Vega, Cygnus the swan flies south across the firmament, with the bright star Deneb glittering in her beak like a diamond she's plucked from an Eastern treasure horde. High above both, ruby-red Arcturus marks the heel of the kindly shepherd Boötes, who drives the stars of spring across the sky.

Orion flees, humbled, below the western horizon; look south in a few weeks and see why. There Scorpius, the deadly scorpion, rises, the bright star Antares burning at its heart. According to legend, Orion claimed that no creature could kill him. Hera, cruel queen of the gods, would tolerate no such boasting and sent a scorpion to vanquish him. Although the hunter smashed Scorpius, in his death throes the scorpion delivered Orion a fatal sting. Zeus placed the opponents at opposite sides of the sky: as one rises, the other sets — and neither is ever seen wholly with the other in the sky. Orion's defeat is the earth's triumph: May is the nail in winter's coffin and the threshold of summer, the final fulfillment of the cuckoo's promise in the early spring.

The Anglo-Saxons called May Thrimilce, because the cows, grown fat on April's new grass, could be milked three times a day. The Romans were the first to call the month May, for reasons still argued over by scholars. Some claim that it was originally named after the Maiores, or majority of the nascent Roman Senate. Others claim, more poetically, that the religion-loving Latins named the month after Maia, their goddess of growth and increase.

As if to echo the riot of new growth during this lovely season, Maia was known by many names: Fatua, Oma, Damia, and, most simply, Bona Dea, the Good

Goddess. Her cult was restricted to women, who held all of her fecund mysteries within their hearts and wombs, and on the first of May a group of Vestal Virgins gathered at the chief magistrate's house to pay Maia due homage. Nobody knows to this day what those rites entailed; men, who really do gossip more than women, and wine, which loosens all lips regardless of gender, were both strictly forbidden. The Romans were so serious about this taboo, and about maintaining the sanctity and secrecy of the cult, that when a drunken magistrate named Clodius crashed one of the ceremonies in 62 B.C., he was put to death and his chief political ally, Cicero, was banished.

An old tradition, also dating from Rome, insists that May is a disastrous month for marriages. The Romans held yet another rite in supplication to the Lemuria, the evil ghosts of the vengeful dead, in May, and the observance probably cast a pall over any ideas of wedded bliss. The taboo against May weddings continued down through the Middle Ages; in northern England, "Marry in May and rue the day" is still a popular saw. An even harsher saying claims that for marriages in May, "all barns die and decay." The fourteenth of May is considered unluckiest of all; any maids who marry on that day, claimed a nineteenth-century Scottish minister, "are stark raving mad." And the fourteenth, believe it or not, is the exact date of the old Roman observance of the

Lemuria. Sometimes the small taboos of the calendar that only schoolchildren or naturally superstitious folk like the Irish still observe can, once understood, send us spinning back down through the generations, until we find ourselves walking the ancient, unfamiliar streets of home.

May 1

Cross-Quarter Day

Beltane, May Day

The wind blows out the gates of day,
The wind blows over the lonely of heart
And the lonely of heart is withered away;
While fairies dance in a place apart,
Shaking their milk-white feet in a ring,
Tossing their milk-white arms in the air.

— W. B. Yeats
The Land of Heart's Desire

Most gentle of ancient days, May Day has all but vanished. Its antipode, Halloween, keeps roaring along, probably because it celebrates those things by which so many are still fascinated: death, spooks, wild nights. May Day celebrates the universal forces that oppose them: life, beneficent spirits, tender evenings in the late spring. The human imagination, which claims to seek solace in the beautiful and the calm, really loves disaster, high drama, Sturm und Drang. So while the streets still careen with imps and devils on the last night of October, May Eve passes with little more fanfare than the whisper of the breeze through young leaves.

It was not always so. In ancient times, young Romans wandered into the fields and spent the first of May dancing and singing in honor of Maia and her consort Floria, goddess of fruits and flowers.

Across Celtic Europe, people celebrated May Day as one of the principal hinges of the year, inaugurating its "light" or summer half. On May Eve, they gathered green branches and flowers that they twined into wreaths or wrapped around sticks, scepters of the season. Girls washed their hair in the dew that settled just before dawn, certain that the spirit of spring would infuse them, and that they would see their true love reflected in the sheen of the heaven-sent water. If Halloween celebrated the certainty of death, May Day celebrated the persistence of life and the possibility of love.

The ancient Irish called May Day Beltane, which can be roughly translated as "the fire of Bel." Bel is a very mysterious character, who seems to have been just about everywhere in the ancient world. Some scholars link him with the horned Celtic deity Cernunnos; others place his origin as far afield as the ancient Middle East, and see the famous Baal of the Old Testament (who demanded that human children be dropped into his cauldronlike mouth) as one of Bel's forerunners. Whoever he was, it is certain that Bel represented the sun, and that his day began as an early pastoral festival accompanying the first turning of the herds out to wild pasture.

Beltane began officially at moonrise on May Eve. The rising moon summoned multitudes of witches, fairies, and the dead to openly walk the land. May Day, like Samhain, was a period of division between one season and the next, and the walls between the worlds grew exceedingly thin. On this night fairies enchanted unwary mortals: but their charms, given the joyful nature of the occasion, were little more than love spells or simple bewilderments. Many reported chasing will-o-the-wisps, or fairy lights, across the countryside, drawn by the beauty of the floating orbs and the unearthly music that accompanied their flight, only to find themselves wide awake and knee-deep in a mountain rill.

The next morning brought Beltane, the day of the sun, the day of renewed fire. As the dawn rose, villagers gathered on hillsides or in village squares. They threw the last of winter's dried wood into a heaping pile and set it on fire. The fires burned all day while the people feasted at their fringes. Robert Fitzgerald could very well have been thinking of these ancient May rites when he admonished readers of his translation of *The Rubaiyat of Omar Khayyam*,

> Awake! And in the fires of spring
> Your winter garment of repentance fling;

> The bird of time has but a little way to flutter
> And the bird is on the wing.

Once again, the Catholic Church had allowed a pagan observance to survive. Under Puritan English rule, the Celtic festival had a harder time. Here is one accurate, if prejudiced, explanation for the persistence of Beltane in Ireland, from the *Gentleman's Magazine* of London, February 1795: "As regards the fire worship of the Irish at this time, no more sources need be sought than the Roman Catholics, who have artfully yielded to the superstitions of the natives, in order to gain and keep up an establishment, grafting Christianity onto pagan rites." Even so, Beltane celebrations lasted well into the nineteenth century, and in remote hamlets in the British Isles they continue to this day.

In medieval Europe, May Day was a widely popular festival day, when fairs were held and feasts enjoyed. After the sun had risen over the fields, the young people of the village gathered in the square and chose a "Queen of the May," a young woman who represented the returning spring.

The selection of a young woman to embody the spring is a hallmark of Celtic culture, in which each shifting season takes on a feminine shape. The winter crone, wise but lethal, ruled winter. By May she had

May Day celebrations around a maypole.

vanished into the loam. From her corpse sprang flowers, to be placed on the brow of a surrogate for a new season.

The Queen of the May, anointed with springwater and wearing a garland of fresh flowers around her head, sat enthroned in a cart pulled through the village by her admirers, most of them men. How little the truly important things in human life change.

Members of the parade carried bunches of flowers or waved May trees, long sticks garlanded with freshly picked flowers. As they marched, the crowd sang hymns to the risen sun, or to the beauty of the Queen of the May. They also chanted implorations for money to the dwellers in the cottages they passed, offering the blessings of the May in exchange for a gift of money, beer, or both.

Finally the skipping, prancing, singing, laughing, garlanded procession arrived at the maypole. This was a very tall piece of wood, usually the polished trunk of a single tree, painted in riotous colors and festooned with flowers.

From the tip of the pole, long ribbons stretched fluttering to the earth, each one a different color. At the foot of the pole, each celebrant took the end of a ribbon in his or her hand and joined in a communal, circular dance. As the ribbons wound down around the pole, the dancers were forced closer and closer together, until the whole young company wound up in a joyous heap.

In some villages, every house in town boasted a maypole in the front yard. Often the maypole was left standing on the village green, serving as a reminder through winter's long weeks of the eventual vernal celebration to come.

The most famous maypoles in history were erected on the Strand, a hustling, bustling London neighborhood that for generations served as the site of public celebrations. The first maypole appeared during the heady reign of Queen Elizabeth I, "Good Bess," who loved the old traditions of her country and undoubtedly took a few spins around the maypole herself. Elizabeth's maypole was toppled and burned by Cromwell's Puritan zealots in 1644. Another, 134 feet high, appeared on the Strand in 1661, during the nationwide celebrations following the restoration of the crown by Charles II. In 1713, badly decayed, it was replaced by another of equal height, a gift to London from a sea captain who had made a fortune in the East Indies.

This last of the Strand maypoles only stood for five years and met a curious, cosmic fate. In 1718 it was carefully removed, having been sold to none other than Sir Isaac Newton. Newton shipped the towering pole to an astronomer friend in Wanstead, who erected it in a park, where this most pagan of artifacts formed the supporting base of the largest telescope in the world.

All of this pleasant May Day activity really had only one purpose: bringing new life into the village. Winter the killer was dead, and the creative energy of the world reborn. How better to celebrate than to transform a town into a forest, a street into a meadowland? The accouterments of the day, the bouquets of flowers, the vines twined around freshly cut switches, the songs and the parades and the young in one another's arms, all had the power to literally "bring in the May": to bestow upon the human population of the town the richness of blossoming nature.

By the dawn of the modern world, May Day had survived its Protestant tribulations and become again wildly popular in England, where it was celebrated as a national field day. All over the country, people flocked to country fairs, where they danced away the afternoon, played games, held archery contests, and drank the first batch of spring ale under brightly painted canopies. During the late Middle Ages, Robin Hood and Maid Marian, two great folk heroes whose story suggests a pagan return to nature, came to preside as Lord and Lady of May. Two handsome youths were chosen to portray the famous couple in forest green, and often the celebration would end with a mock wedding between the two.

This playful custom replaced an older May Day tradition in which the Queen of the May was ceremonially wedded to the Green Man of the Woods, a figure dressed in nothing but vegetation who emerged from the forest to woo his springtime bride and restore the fecundity of the earth.

Maid Marian was the last of the May Day figures to

assume the mantle of the ancient goddesses of the spring. She brought on the wrath of the Puritans, whose displeasure is evident in the following complaint, registered by a minister who attended a May Day pageant in the early eighteenth century: "These are in their origin bad; they are shamefully abused, having in them piping and dancing, and Maid Marian coming into the church at the time of prayer to move laughter and kissing in the church, and they justly deserve to be called profane, riotous and disorderly."

Thanks to such disapproval, and the condemnation of all things natural by the advent of the Industrial Revolution, May Day gradually faded away. By the twentieth century, it had been stripped of its pagan trappings and appropriated by Socialists as the International Workers' Day. The old night of spring is now famous not for its bucolic origins but for its political symbolism. All of the old figures of the day — the Queen of the May and her courtier the Green Man, Robin and Marian, the maypole and its dancing attendants, the mock battles between winter and spring, have vanished from the Western imagination.

And yet, and yet . . .

On the first Sunday of May, at Catholic churches across Europe and America, parishioners assemble outside the sanctuary. Each bears a candle. They stand in silence until the priest arrives with a burning taper. He holds it before the altar boys and girls, so that they might bend to catch the sacred flame. They, in turn, light every candle that surrounds them. Soon, in spite of the fact that the glory of the morning sun pales them into so many impotent and unnecessary gleams, several hundred candles burn.

From within the sanctuary, a girl, usually about fourteen, emerges. Dressed in radiant, bridal white, she holds in her hands a bouquet of spring flowers: hyacinths, pansies, lilies.

The priest blesses her. The girl leads the congregation in procession along the parish grounds. Prayers are spoken and sung. The priest from time to time casts the asperses; tendrils of holy water spin and fall on blades of grass and upturned faces as the church boundaries are reached and sanctified.

Finally the processional halts before a statue of the Virgin Mary. The May Queen, as she is called, now purified by water, prayer, song, flowers, and the beams of the wholly resurrected sun, gently places her bouquet upon the brow of Mary: she who intercedes, kindest of saints, the queen of Heaven.

All kneel and sing a song of praise to her, whom their furthest ancestors would surely recognize. In spite of modernity's triumph and the defeat of nature, despite the zealotry and arrogance that did her older sisters in, Mary — as did Isis, Maia, Floralia, and Marian — fulfills her duty as the last surviving goddess of the West, and brings in the May.

June

At the Height of Glory

When I consider everything that grows
Holds in perfection but a little moment
That this huge stage presenteth nought but shows
Whereon the stars in secret influence comment;
When I perceive that men as plants increase,
Cheered and chequed even by the self-same sky,
Vaunt in their youthful sap, at height decrease,
And wear their brave state out of memory;
Then the conceit of this inconstant stay
Sets you most rich in youth before my sight,
Where wasteful time debateth with decay,
To change your day of youth to sullied night;
And all in war with Time for love of you,
As he takes from you, I engraft you new.

— William Shakespeare
"Sonnet XV"

 is herald roars silenced by the halt of the sun,
Leo now dives toward the northern horizon.
Directly above, three bright stars form the

summer triangle that will shine throughout the rest of
the season: Vega, in the lyre of Orpheus; Deneb, the
tail feather of Cygnus; and, last to rise, Altair, the sharp
eye of Aquila, the eagle. All three of these beautiful
stars bear Arab names, for it was the Muslim cultures of
the early Middle Ages that kept astronomy alive after
the collapse of Rome.

Vega means "vulture," a bird that the Arabs thought
Lyra resembled. They, like the Greeks, saw in the wide
cross of Cygnus a celestial swan, and dubbed her brightest star Deneb, which means, simply, "tail." Altair, the
brightest star of Aquila and one of the brightest in the
entire night sky, is Arabic for "eagle." Low in southern
skies, bright red Antares, the last of summer's stellar jewels, marks the deadly heart of Scorpio as he creeps along
the horizon, seeking Orion, the prey he will never find.

In his ribald masterpiece *The Metamorphosis*, the Roman
poet and fantasist Ovid claims that the month was
named after Juno, queen of the gods. Modern scholars,
however, who naturally know more about Roman history than a man of genius who lived in its midst, insist
that June is actually derived from the Juniores, the
lower branch of the first Roman legislature.

Ovid's explanation makes more poetic and, ultimately, more practical sense. Juno, the queen of the gods,
endured a miserable marriage to her husband Jupiter, who
fathered not only the gods but also an army of illegiti-

Leo.

mate children. Juno, then, did not look kindly on marital infidelity, and often punished her husband's mortal lovers by transforming them into beasts, shipwrecking them on desolate islands, or cursing them to give birth to monsters. Young Roman brides, perhaps a little worried about their husband's wandering eyes, often prayed to Juno to make their men walk the straight and narrow. That is why, since Roman times, June has been considered a lucky month for weddings. And the full moon of June, sacred to both Juno and Venus, the silver goddess of love, was considered the luckiest time of all the year for a march down the aisle.

June brings the summer in, but it also marks a decisive decision of the sun that will result in summer's end. Throughout the winter and the spring, the ritual year has been dedicated to calling the sun back from his southern exile. In June, that journey is completed. At the summer solstice, the sun reaches its most northern point in the sky, and, astronomically, summer begins. But no sooner does the sun climb to glory than it slowly begins to move south again.

Although June traditionally opens the happy summer season, the astronomical basis of the calendar makes the month a prediction of tomorrow as much as a celebration of today. The sun hangs high in the sky, shines forth the brightest and longest beams of the year, then, like a lover grown suddenly uncertain, slowly wanders away. Astronomically, June inaugurates summer; what it promises, even as the corn grows and the swallows dart happily above the blooming meadows and the ocean calls children to bathe in her bracing waters, is inevitable winter.

June 24

Quarter Day

Summer Solstice, Midsummer Night

I know a bank where the wild thyme blows
Where oxlips and the nodding violet grows,
Quite over-canopied with luscious woodbine,
With sweet musk-roses, and with eglantine;
There sleeps Titania sometime in the night,
Lull'd in these flowers with dances and delight.

— William Shakespeare
A Midsummer Night's Dream

A night of magic, mystery, and sex, Midsummer Night was for centuries the most important and widespread annual festival in Europe: the great revel of the year, when people cast all inhibitions aside amid flowers and rumpled clothes.

As the Germanic peoples — Goths, Franks, and Anglo-Saxons — gained control of the continent, they brought their midsummer festival to prominence. Early in the first millennium, the church appropriated the old midsummer festival, renaming it Saint John's Day, and as usual allowed the pagan rites to continue. June 24 is still celebrated in the Catholic Church as Saint John the Baptist's Day; another Christian veneer slipped over a pagan memory. In Celtic countries that fell under Germanic sway, Midsummer Night subsumed Beltane, although the celebrations were in many ways identical. In Ireland, in fact, it is said that Saint Patrick switched the festival from Beltane to Saint John's Day to bring Ireland more into keeping with mainstream continental practices.

On Midsummer Eve, the invisible beings with whom we share the world are allowed to reveal themselves and roam, unmasked and unashamed, through the pleasant night. Witch, fairy, or walking dead, the creatures of our highest and darkest imaginations crowd the fields, perch on the stiles, rustle in the thick summer trees, meet by moonlight. Under their reign, all magic, white or black, good or evil, petty or terrifying, triples in strength.

Summer means growth, fecundity, the sweat of labor under the midday sun and the sweat of passion beneath the ripe moon. The natural world brews her most potent magic during this high tide of teeming life, and plants plucked beneath the midnight moon on Midsummer Eve double their effect and keep fresh twice as long as others. And plants named after the saint of the day, "the herbs of Saint John," have an especially potent effect, if harvested at midnight or the exact stroke of noon. Saint John's-wort, hawkweed, vervain, orpine, mullen, mistletoe (again we meet this remarkable plant, sacred to Celt and German alike), even wormwood; they all serve many uses.

If burned, they prevent fire. Hawkweed hung from the rafters sends the rats scurrying away and even dismays the midnight witch, come to steal the sleeping babe. Saint John's-wort, brewed and drunk as a tea, calms the household and soothes family quarrels. Divining rods cut on this night never fail, midsummer dew gives sight to the blind, and the dreams that visit those who sleep outdoors beneath the vaulting moon come true.

In northern Europe, the Wild Hunt is on the loose, as summer showers and rolling thunder track the progress of Odin and his band across the sky. Some Teutonic tribes sacrificed young children to the rough gods by drowning them in rivers on Midsummer Night. A more general — and gentler — tradition maintained that water gathered at midsummer acted as a cure-all. Across the length and breadth of Europe, from Germany to Spain, from Ireland to Greece, people waited until the stroke of twelve, then headed for the nearest stream, river, or pool, where they stripped naked and bathed together unashamed. The spirit of midsummer, it was said, would infuse them, bringing them health and good luck throughout the year. This delightful ritual undoubtedly produced a great many March babies.

*   *   *

The signal ritual of Midsummer's Day involved a re-creation of the sun in the form of bonfires. The ancients understood that midsummer was the triumph of the sun, but also the beginning of his long defeat during the waning of the year. In order to hearten him on his journey into darkness, people set fires ablaze on the hilltops. These bonfires, mini suns, could also give a bit of the burning orb's power to mortals below before it began to wane.

Everything about these fires was sacred. Cattle were driven through the flames to purify them; their drivers huddled close by to breathe in the acrid smoke. Newlyweds danced at the edges of the fires, and at a signal leaped through them arm in arm to the blaring music of pipe and fiddle.

Young children would spend the whole day weaving vines into disks, some as small as a discus, others as large as a table. They then lit these small suns on fire and hurled them into the sky or rolled them down the hillsides. Battles were fought between summer and winter. Effigies representing Winter, Illness, Old Age, even Death, were covered with pitch, hoisted from gallows, and set ablaze. No matter how frenzied these celebrations became, all who participated were careful to carry a burning branch or taper, lit from a bonfire or a flaming disk, back to their homes. There they carefully set a fire in the hearth and fired it with the sacred flame. No matter how hard the winter to come, summer's strength now abided in the heart of the home.

As Shakespeare realized, to the delight of generations of theatergoers, this night, like the Eve of May that it supplanted, is about love. Lovers joined hands across the midsummer bonfire, tossed flowers across the flames to one another, or leaped through it together. Lonely hearts practiced divinations of all sorts to try and discover their future brides or grooms. In Scandinavia, little girls placed midsummer flowers under their pillows to induce dreams of love and ensure that they would come true.

An ancient folk belief, common throughout the British Isles, insists that if a lonely maid fasts all the day on midsummer, and at midnight sets her cottage table with cakes, cheese, and ale, her future husband will appear at the gate and join her.

A folktale only, bred undoubtedly of simple rustic minds. But how I delight to imagine them there, as the soft candlelight flickers along the whitewashed cottage walls: a woman in the first flush of her beauty, and a man with a spark in his eye. They share their modest feast, speaking softly about the weather or the cattle, or perhaps, as the ale and the hint of love work their spell, about their secret dreams. The candle burns low. A scent of wild thyme drifts in through the open sash. The wise old moon plays chaperone with one eye closed. The summer night pauses, and all the gods on Olympus look down in envy, as a young man's hand finds its way across the table to clasp that of his charmer.

Summer

A roadside inn this summer Saturday:
The doors are open to the wide warm air,
The parlor, whose old window views the bay,
Garnished with cracked delph full of flowers fair
From the fields round, and whence you see the glare
Fall heavy on the hot slate roofs and o'er
The wall's tree shadows drooping in the sun.
Now rumbles slowly down the dusty street
The lazy drover's clattering cart; and crows
Fainter through afternoon the cock; with hoes
Tan-faced harvest folk trudge in the heat:
The neighbors at their shady doors swept clean,
Gossip, and with cool eve fresh scents of wheat,
Grasses and leaves, come from the meadows green.

— Thomas Caulfield Irwin
"A Roadside Inn This Summer Saturday"

July

Caesura

he arctic bears tramp the summer night and fill the skies with their happy roars. Between them twines Draco, the great dragon of the north. Like Ursa Major and her cub, Draco is a circumpolar constellation; his length is so great that he can only been seen in his entirety at this time of the year. Far longer even than Draco, spangling the night sky with an infinity of stars, the Milky Way runs the length of heaven. Cygnus the swan wings his stately way above the celestial highway, announcing high summer. Yet already a messenger of autumn has appeared: Pegasus, the great horse, spreads his wings above the horizon, warning us that no summer can last forever.

Originally called Quintillus, "five," by the Romans, July was named after Julius Caesar by his adopted son Gaius, who later, as the emperor Augustus, would have a month named after him as well. The Romans loved their slain dictator Julius, and the celebrations that met the announcement of the month's new name lasted for three straight days. Caesar's fame only grew through the centuries, and the name of July stuck.

In medieval England, July marked the advent of festivals where ale was the main drink. Generally held on college campuses or parish grounds, these parties raised money for the hosting institution and became known as Church or College Ales. They resembled May Day festivals: a king and queen of the fair were elected, along with lords and ladies. Jesters and fools cavorted about, along with pantomime horses and costumed giants striding about on stilts. These community fairs, with their veneer of civic duty, were really simple celebrations of the season. July meant hard work in the fields, but it also held long, warm days and starry nights, when people could stroll outdoors, smell the hedges and the flowers, and generally enjoy life. The Ales lasted through the Middle Ages, until Puritanism snuffed them out. But not forever.

In the rebellious America of 1776, the release of the Declaration of Independence brought about an instant resurrection of the Old World summer party. Now that the colonists had their own country to toast, they reverted to the ways of their ancestors with a passion. The Fourth of July became a day of patriotic speeches, parades, and firework displays, events punctuated by the consumption of endless platters of food and gallons of beer.

American children ran through the late-summer twilight with poppers and sparklers. They played at hoops and marbles, or snuck off behind the house to share in a bucket of sweet, cool beer. Older Americans danced or had pleasant conversation celebrating the determined liberties of the young nation. The oldest folk, who knew what they had gained but also what they had lost, toasted their new country with a deep solemnity, and perhaps wished in secret for just one more taste of the beer brewed during other Julys, long ago across the sea, in a country that had borne them, but would never again be home.

In July, the year reaches its midpoint and summer reaches its zenith. From December 21, the shortest day of the year, until June 21, the longest, the calendar has both reiterated and predicted the return of the sun to northern climes. Now the sun, having returned from winter's precipice, prepares for another journey south.

At this moment, as if it knows that a long hard descent lies just ahead, the calendar pauses. During July, no major pagan or Christian feast falls. The ritual calendar will recommence in August, when days begin to noticeably shorten, and the cycle of the great autumn festivals — Lughnasa, Halloween, and Thanksgiving — begins. July is a breath in the midst of the year, a vacation from ritual.

In ancient Greece, the Etesian wind blew during

July, a hot caress that led Greeks down to the seashore. It might be hard to imagine Plato or Sophocles lolling on the beach like any sun worshipper at Malibu or the Riviera, but they did. They dozed on the white sand and swam in the Aegean's cobalt water. After the fall of dark, they lit bonfires on the sand, roasted lamb on spits, drank wine, and wove wonderful tales beneath the summer stars. In spite of the ages that separate us, the Greeks probably thought of this time of year in the same way that we do: as a hope that summer might last forever, waiting at the edge of the sea where children laugh, gulls chatter, and sandpipers scuttle in the hot sun.

August

The Gateway to Splendid Beauties

he Dipper now hangs upright in the sky, bearing between its claws its precious water during the hot nights. Unseen during the night, but ascendant in the sky from dawn to dusk, the Dog Star, Sirius, keeps company with the sun. The ancients, who knew this, thought that bright Sirius lent his heat to that of Sol, and brought the sweltering "dog days" of August to unhappy men below.

Below Cygnus, the great square of Pegasus rises in the northeast. The winged horse, who had sprung from the headless trunk of the Medusa after Perseus slew her, points to another figure from the Perseus myth; from the lower left of Pegasus's square run two lines of stars that form Andromeda, the princess that Perseus saved from the sea monster. And indeed, the hero himself appears, rising low in the northeast, a warning that autumn is approaching fast.

*   *   *

The month of August is named after Gaius Julius Caesar Octavianus, better known to history as Caesar Augustus; he who, as emperor, ordered that the whole world be taxed. Since the Roman taxes had to be paid in the city of the subject's birth, Augustus unwittingly sent a Jewish carpenter named Joseph, along with his pregnant wife Mary, on a journey from Nazareth to Bethlehem, where Joseph had been born. Had Augustus known what would come of that journey, he probably would have revoked the tax.

Augustus had actually been born in September, but he preferred the month of Sextilis (as August was originally called) because of the luck that it had brought him through his life. In Sextilis he was admitted to the consulate; during another Sextilis he conquered Egypt; and in the glorious Sextilis of 43 B.C. he defeated Mark Antony during the naval battle of Actium and won the Civil Wars, the Roman Empire, and immortality. Soon thereafter, by decree of the Roman Senate, Sextilis ceased to be, replaced in name by that of the mighty Augustus Caesar, who donned his purple tunic, took to his alabaster throne, and bowed before the adulation of his distinguished patrician slaves.

The Romans called August "the forerunner of splendid beauties," a month hinting of the fall to come. Although the sun still blazes like a furnace, the days grow shorter as it drops a little earlier each evening. On most August days, haze dwindles distance, and muggy air settles on the land like a blanket. But there is always one dawn in August that brings a cool breeze flapping the window shade. The light has changed, and the birds sing a new tune; they sound happy and a little frantic, like kids who are about to travel.

In August, the last of summer's bounties arrive: silver corn and summer squash, lobster and the year's fattest crabs, peppers of every variety, and of course tomatoes. We say good-bye to the sun's dominion by feasting at picnic tables beneath the waning summer triangle, remembering the small events of the past season: days at the beach, heat waves, notable thunderstorms, midnight laughter. During the last days of August, we relish her gifts while observing no command of the calendar save one: that summer is like a child waiting to grow up, and that the journey, so long anticipated, should perhaps next year be enjoyed more fully, with a few more trips to the pool and a bit less fussing about the heat. After all, it is over before we know it.

August 1

Cross-Quarter Day

Lughnasa, Lammas

Lughnasa was an important Celtic festival of games and dance that marked the advent of the autumn season. Although it had disappeared on the continent by the late Middle Ages, the festival survived in isolated Ireland down to the twentieth century. *Lughnasa* means, roughly, "the wedding of Lugh." The Irish believed that on this day the god Lugh married the beautiful goddess Eriu, the "sovereignty of Ireland." Lugh was the hero-god of Irish mythology, a kind of Hercules character who saved damsels from monsters and shielded mortals against the ravages of malign gods.[9] Most importantly, he also represented the sun.

Eriu, for her part, symbolized all of Ireland. Her dominion stretched from the towering cliffs of the Aran Islands to the verdant Wicklow Hills skirting the Irish Sea. "Erin," in fact, which is still used by Irish and English speakers alike as a name for Ireland, means "the land of

---

[9] I strongly suspect that the waning American expression "big lug" derives from this fellow.

Eriu." Eriu, like the island she embodied, was at the height of her summer beauty at Lughnasa. Alas, soon after her marriage to the sun god, Eriu's loveliness began to fade with the onset of fall; by winter she would be transformed into the dreadful winter hag, the Cailleac.

Lughnasa provides an insight into how literally the Celts and their Irish descendants regarded the natural world as a divine female. The Celts celebrated Lughnasa as a real wedding, followed by a night of passionate lovemaking between the gods. And the epithalamion sung by their mortal worshippers bore precious fruit; exactly nine months from Lughnasa, Beltane (May Day) fell, when Lugh's seed and Eriu's egg, carried by the goddess during the long winter, emerged as the newborn spring. At that time, according to some early medieval accounts, the kiss of Lugh transformed the hag of winter into a radiant beauty. Memories of this mystical wedding survive in Ireland, where August is still considered the luckiest of all months to find a future husband or wife.

For centuries, a great Lughnasa dance was held at Teltown on the river Boyne, where a grassy mound, probably the remains of a Neolithic temple, still marks the site of the festivities. The fair featured much drinking and dancing, athletic contests, merchants hawking goods from tented stalls, and of course (this being an Irish event) nonstop music.

The climax of the fair came when a large group of single men gathered on one side of Teltown mound, and a group of single women collected on the other. A witness described the ensuing events: "To the flourish of whistles and the clamor of drums, matchmakers dashed between these anxious armies, making marriage contracts." Another account claims that in "the hollow of the fair," nuptials had been performed since pagan times. Even in the late nineteenth century, men and women would follow the ancient call of Lugh to Teltown on the first of August, seeking husbands and brides.

The idea of a god marrying the earth to ensure future fecundity has been accompanied throughout Western history by a similar notion that the king bears within his own physical being the welfare of the land. This idea infuses the Arthurian legends, wherein an ailing king holds the secret of the Holy Grail, the chalice from which Christ drank at the Last Supper. The knight errant Galahad, after much wandering and disillusionment, discovers the secret of the Grail: the land and the king are one. No sooner does Galahad whisper this bit of simple wisdom in the king's ear than Arthur is restored to vigor, and the land itself, which had become a blasted wilderness during the king's decline, is restored to life.

A late medieval manuscript describing Lughnasa customs emulates this story. At Teltown, a king named Lug Scimaig held a great feast to celebrate his "wedding of the sovranty," that is, not his marriage to a woman, but to the kingship itself, to the stewardship of the land

and its people. An eleventh-century manuscript finds another Lug married to a great fairy queen referred to as "the sovranty of the country."

The fact that Eriu was slowly transformed over the years into a fairy queen only points more sharply at her once-divine stature. Teltown apparently took its name from Tailtiu, Lugh's foster mother, who was buried on the spot. Lug instituted the games to memorialize her. This folk explanation seems to have arisen after the true meaning of the word *Lughnasa* and the festival had been forgotten, and the role of the pagan god Lugh had been transferred to mortal kings.

Ultimately, Lughnasa was Christianized into *Lammas*, a word derived from the Old English words for "loaf" and "mass." Even under the influence of the church, the festival retained most of its pagan elements, celebrating the gathering of the harvest and the coming of the fall. The church holiday specifically celebrated the ripening of apples and winter wheat, the latter being, according to tradition, made into loaves and blessed by the church. Lammas was also a day of accounts: in Scotland, tenant farmers took their first grain harvests to the landlords to pay the rent.

Once again, the calendar is predictive of changes in the natural world. Marriage between the sun and the earth is made while the light still blazes — insurance against the distant but coming winter that coincides with the approaching harvest. When Eriu and her consort finally, with dawn of the modern world, left the hill of Teltown, they took away with them an idea that gave meaning to the lives of generations of people closer to the earth than we can ever dream of being: that marriage could be made between the sun and the earth while his light burned bright, and that that light could be carried through the long months of winter as a secret child named Spring.

September

Intimations of Mortality

The summer was over at last, and nobody could deny any longer that the autumn was definitely there. It was that rather sad time of year when for the first time in many months the fine old sun still blazes away in a cloudless sky, but does not warm you, and the hoar-frosts and mists and the winds begin to stir their faint limbs at morning and evening, as the sap of winter vigor remembers itself in the corpses which brave summer slew.

— T. H. White
The Sword in the Stone

he stars of summer reach their final apogee in the sky; one last parade through the warm and pleasant evenings before the winds of autumn hurry them from the celestial scene. Vega and Deneb shine directly overhead, as if boasting of their eventual return. Altair casts his baleful eye toward the south. There, the "watery" constellations can be seen rising above the horizon. The Greeks thought that below the equator lay a great and limitless stream of ocean, and named some of the constellations they glimpsed briefly at this time of year for their association with water, as in Pisces the fish and Aquarius the water-bearer.

Farther south, and invisible to those who live above 38 degrees of latitude, is the enormous constellation of Argo Navis, named after the ship that carried Jason and the Argonauts on their adventures. Sky watchers later broke up this huge constellation to form three smaller concentrations of stars: Carina, the keel; Vela, the sail; and Puppis, the poop deck.

Although named after the famous *Argo*, the great starry vessel of the sky was also said to have been the first ship ever sailed, and was placed in the sky by Zeus as a celebration of man's nautical prowess. In the early autumn, if you live south of the Mid-Atlantic states, watch for Canopus, one of the brightest stars in the sky, on the southern horizon. It forms the tip of Carina, Argo's celestial keel, steering the ship ever southward. While autumn comes to the north with fluttering leaves and chill breezes, the great ship of heaven follows the sun.

Our ninth month, along with the three that follow it, still bears its fallacious Latin name: September, seven. Although the Roman Senate made innumerable attempts to rename September, October, November, and December, the common people stubbornly insisted on calling them by their old outdated names, as we still do.

The Anglo-Saxons called September Gerstmonath, or "barley month," the season when they gathered the barley from which they brewed their October ale. They also called September Haerfestmonath, "holy month," because at the time of the autumn equinox they held a solemn religious festival to mark the waning of the year with chants, torchlit processions, and sacrifices. By the time of Charlemagne, the month was simply called "Harvest."

In Europe and later in America, farmers used the light of the full moon nearest the autumn equinox to work late into the night, gathering the harvest. This was a terribly important business, and whole villages headed out into the fields to work until the ripe moon set. Young people, unaccustomed to working after dark, actually looked forward to the night's labor. It gave them a chance to meet their sweethearts in the silver light, to chat and flirt as they labored. When the harvest moon finally sank, everyone gathered in barns or open glades to celebrate. They played music and danced, opened the last keg of summer's yellow wheat beer, allowed themselves an evening of fun after hard work. Dancing surely led to kissing, just as every decent instinct in the race still invites young lovers to meet by the light of the harvest moon.

*   *   *

Just as there always comes a wet night in March when the winter finally dies, so too September delivers the last day of summer. It might be a hot one under a strong sun, thick with sweat, hayseed, and mown grass, the scents of summer's labor. After the fall of dark, everything changes. The air stills and settles, and turns cool enough to make people shut their windows halfway. Crickets slow their song. Owls, sluggish until now, quicken their silent flight. Stars that only the night before sat plump in the thick atmosphere now shine like hard jewels against the deepening blue, and the moon, when it rises, looks like a galleon plying the cold sea of night.

September 20–21

Quarter Day

Autumnal Equinox, Cerealia, Harvest Home

Thou comest, Autumn, heralded by the rain,
With banners, by great gales incessant fanned,
Brighter than brightest silks of Samarcand,
And stately oxen harnessed to thy wain!
Thou standest, like imperial Charlemagne,
Upon thy bridge of gold; thy royal hand
Outstretched with benedictions o'er the land,
Blessing the farms through all thy vast domain!
Thy shield is the red harvest moon, suspended
So long beneath the heaven's o'er-hanging eaves;
Thy steps are by the farmer's prayers attended;
Like flames upon an altar shine the sheaves;
And, following thee, in thy ovation splendid,
Thine almoner, the wind, scatters the golden leaves!

— Henry Wadsworth Longfellow
"Autumn"

The old harvest festivals that used to crowd around the
autumnal equinox have been displaced by two other fall

celebrations, Halloween and Thanksgiving. Up until the twentieth century, September parades celebrating the last gathering of the summer's harvest were common throughout the American Midwest and across Europe. All that remains in our modern society is a collection of folklore and memory; the harvest is now a simple economic fact, and the equinox now passes with a brief mention by the meteorologist on the five o'clock news.

For generations of farmers, the equinox was one of the chief feasts of the year. Depending on where you lived, it signaled either the onset of the harvest or its close. In either case, it marked a time when the crops so assiduously cared for during the growing season began to yield up their bounty. Summer made the forests and meadows teem with food: berries and fruit for foragers, game for hunters, grass for grazing cows. The blessings of the earth lay within easy reach. Summer also nourished life beneath the soil: wheat and rye and other grains, all waiting for the days when the sun faded southward and the fruit dried up, the game wandered off and the grass grew brittle and stale.

In the days before modern commercial farming, grains and tubers planted in the spring only came to maturity at the close of summer. Once harvested, they could be milled into flour and baked into bread. We take a loaf of bread for granted these days; it is the most basic, and least expensive, food on the supermarket shelf. For people who had to be self-sustaining, a loaf of bread cut in January meant life. And because it came from grain that had been nurtured and nourished by the rays of the sun, bread contained the energy of its creator. Bread is still the central symbol in religious rites like communion, and for a very good reason. Bread is the stored energy of the universe, waiting to be consumed in winter, waiting to bring life.

Harvest festivals predate language, and they probably began as a way of thanking the gods for a successful crop. While we would not recognize many of the plants harvested by ancient people — they had marvelous Semitic names like smelt or kamut — the ceremonies that attended their reaping have been reiterated down through the ages. The Sumerians chose a queen of the harvest every year, who served as the chief priestess of the harvest goddess; five thousand years later, many midwestern cities still crown a corn queen on Main Street. People in ancient Greece and Rome did much the same thing. The harvest meant sustenance through the winter, as the grains collected were ground into flour and stored away, to be baked into cake and breads as the need arose. Nor was this activity merely physical; it was also a profound demonstration of the earth's steady cycles and of the bounty of the gods, who had taught human beings to sow and to reap.

The most famous of ancient harvest rituals began as a myth explaining the perverse cycles of bounty and want attending the natural world and ended up being a

Pomona, Roman goddess of the harvest.

kind of social register of Greco-Roman civilization. Every September, from the earliest days of Greek history until the waning days of the Roman Empire, the little town of Eleusis, about twelve miles west of Athens, played host to the powerful and famous. Athletic stars, poets, playwrights, orators, philosophers, and eventually emperors came to the hamlet on the plains of Attica to celebrate the renowned Eleusinian mysteries.

The Greeks held the city of Eleusis and its surrounding plains as most sacred. They had been the site of one of mythology's most important dramas, a story that explained no less a cosmic event than the changing of the seasons: the rape of Persephone.

Demeter, the daughter of Zeus (yes, another one), was the Greek goddess of nature. She oversaw the growth of animals and plants, and the first few centuries of her reign allowed earth to enjoy perpetual summer. All and everything grew, and nothing died.

Demeter's daughter, Persephone, was the most beautiful creature in the world. Day after day Persephone and her mother roamed the valleys and the meadows, calling flowers to bloom and trees to leaf. On one unlucky afternoon, while her mother lingered in a nearby wood, Persephone wandered alone into a field of high wheat near Eleusis. There the grim god Hades, lord of the dead, beheld her. Overcome by lust, he swept the maiden into his ebony chariot and whisked her into the underworld.

Demeter searched for Persephone in vain. Finally, exhausted and enraged, she raised her fists to Zeus and uttered a terrible curse: So long as she was without her daughter, the sun would weaken. The winds would sweep like ice across the plains. No bird would call nor flower bloom. All would become icy desolation. No sooner had she spoken than the first cold wind ever felt on earth began to blow, and the first dying leaf settled to the ground.

Demeter stumbled into Eleusis, where she collapsed at a well entwined with flowers already wilting under her curse. The daughters of the king found her there, took her in, and comforted her. As a reward for their kindness, she requested that the people of the town build her a temple, from whose marble confines she would protect them, as they had protected her. And there she stayed, mourning her lost child and giving the little town something very much to brag about, a resident goddess.

Zeus grew very afraid that the earth would perish under Demeter's eternal winter and commanded Hades to let Persephone go. But the girl had made a great mistake; starved, she had gnawed six seeds of the pomegranate, the food of the dead. These tiny seeds imbued her with the curse of Hades. She was henceforth doomed to return to the underworld as Hades' queen for exactly the number of months that equaled the seeds she had consumed. Six seeds; six months.

Persephone emerged from the darkness and fell

into her mother's embrace. Spring returned, but the deal had been struck.

Thus the Greeks justified the seasons. While Demeter and her daughter wandered the earth together, flowers bloomed beneath their feet and spring ripened into summer. After six months of joy, Persephone returned to her cold master. Demeter mourned, and the earth died.

And Hades, death, had caused it all; death who was death before death even existed, a god in a world that did not know him; in the land of the eternal sun he waited in the shadows. The wisdom, oddness, and perfect, irrational rationality of the Greeks still justifies that which makes little sense, and perfect sense, and no sense at all. To have Death abduct a woman who will be the very cause of death because of his abducting her leads us into mazes that, as the Greeks used to say, only a Greek could reason out. In this myth we discover some of the true roots of both poetry and mathematics.

And that may be the key to the Eleusinian mysteries, that confluence of logic and dream, myth, and reality. The Greeks were as fond of logical conundrums and philosophical absurdities as they were of hot meat on the spit and writhing bodies in the bed. Maybe, on the plain of Eleusis, they saw and felt both.

In any event, the facts of the ceremony are scarce.

Initiates trooped out of the little town waving burning sheaves of wheat, reciting prayers dedicated to

Demeter and Persephone. They walked in procession to the cave that tradition claimed to be the shaft into the underworld through which Hades had carried the maid. They entered the grotto, their torches casting eerie shadows on the limestone walls. Then they vanished. The next morning, they reappeared in town, exhausted and elated.

Beyond these very simple reports, we know nothing. The cult swore all inductees into silence on the pain of death and — absolutely, remarkably — every one of them (including such renowned blabbermouths as Socrates) kept mum. Both Plato and Marcus Aurelius, men separated by centuries of time, reported that the Eleusinian mysteries changed their lives. This place seems the real thing, a kind of Zen temple of old Greece; a subterranean arena of enlightenment offering epiphanies that, even in a country famous for talkers, awed those who entered into silence.

Romans celebrated the festival of the Cerealia at the equinox, praising Ceres, the Roman incarnation of Demeter.[10] The tradition survived in Europe, where the

---

[10]She still survives, in no less a place than the dome of the U.S. Capitol. In 1865 the Italian artist Constantino Brumidi decorated the dome's oculus with an enormous fresco depicting (along with George Washington rising into the heavens and Neptune laying the transatlantic telegraph cable) Ceres riding across wheat fields athwart a McCormick reaper.

harvest was celebrated with an elaborate set of ceremonies that varied from hamlet to hamlet.

In England, the final ritual of reaping was called Harvest Home. As twilight fell over the last flurry of work, two boys headed out into the fields and carried back the final sheaf of harvested wheat. This was the "spirit of the corn." This custom leads us back to the fields of the Sumerians, who would choose a ritualized prize of the crop upon which to cast spells and prayers for a bountiful harvest. Now the wheat was wrapped in a dress, decked with ribbons, and tied to a pole. The children sang a chant: "Harvest Home! Harvest Home!"

That signaled the end of labor. Farmers and their families trooped through the stubbled fields, holding aloft their maiden of wheat, blowing horns, and dancing jigs in the flying straw. They carried the little goddess to a barn, where they raised her high in the rafters to watch over the ensuing dance.

In Scotland, the harvest maiden took on the form of the hag or witch, presiding over the year's death. Again we meet the Cailleac, assuming now the image of the summer's last crop and the winter to come, linking the cycles of life and death. These female totems, known by a thousand different names — corn mother, harvest maiden, rye woman, barley girl — became the symbol of the culmination of the harvest, and of the certitude held in the hearts of people throughout European history that the earth was, in the end, a woman.

This is a fact to be remembered, even though the autumn equinox and its harvest now pass with little notice, even though troops of weary laborers marching under a bobbing mannequin of calico and straw no more pass by. The world remembers; the fields remember. When September comes, we too should remember those families of long ago trooping through the fields, and we should seek the orange disk of the harvest moon, herald of autumn's glories. Demeter has begun to wander, searching and searching for the daughter she will not hold again until the dawn of another spring. Being a goddess, she has a keen sense of beauty, and will make sure that her grief becomes nothing less than a paean to lost Persephone: ineluctable October.

Autumn

Now westlin winds and slaughtering guns
Brin Autumn's pleasant weather
The moorcock springs on whirring wings
Among the blooming heather
Now waving grain, wild o'er the plain
Delights the weary farmer
And the moon shines bright as I rove at night
To muse upon my charmer.

— Robert Burns
"Now Westlin Winds"

October

The Dead

We close our eyes and go spinning back to those old haunted falls, the happy-sad bittersweet drunk Octobers. What needs to be discharged is the intolerable tenderness of the past, the past gone and grieved over and never made sense of.

— Walker Percy
Love in the Ruins

s the summer triangle drops, visible now only in the early evening, the royal stars of autumn rise to replace them: Perseus, the great hero, with his bride, lovely Andromeda, and her mother, Queen Cassiopeia. Below the royal family, Aldebaran, the bright red eye of Taurus the bull, gleams like a distant ruby. Above Aldebaran shine the Pleiades, those gorgeous attendants to so many of the year's changes, lovelier still for being impossible quite to see. We have met them so many times during the course of our journey, the Seven Sisters, the gleaming princesses of the night sky. No wonder that the ancients thought of them as women, bearing royal mysteries in their elusive appearances. Women's hearts, after all, are as unknowable as the final configuration of the Seven Sisters. All that we can do is catch them from the corner of our eye, and hope that they look back.

High in the southern sky, another character from the Perseus myth, the winged horse Pegasus, prances amid the stars. This magnificent horse was born of the blood of the Medusa after Perseus had beheaded her. Mounting Pegasus, Perseus flew off to use the Medusa's head, which turned all that beheld it to stone, to defeat the monster Ceteus, the whale, who also rises into sky at this time of year. Thus did he win the hand of Andromeda, who was to be sacrificed to Ceteus before Perseus's timely arrival.

Athena, the goddess of wisdom, was said to have tamed Pegasus and brought him to her palace at Mount Helicon. There, with a single mighty kick of his hind leg, Pegasus shattered a spur of the mountain. From the new crevasse flowed the bracing and lovely Hippocrene stream, subsequently blessed by Athena and made sacred to the muses. Greeks considered the stream to be the source of poetic inspiration, as is the month over which mighty Pegasus presides.

*   *   *

October means "eight" in Latin. For centuries after the Romans had changed their calendar and made October the tenth month, they attempted to give it a new name. In the first century A.D., the senate decreed that the month be named after the valiant general Germanicus (who had been given that title in commemoration of his stunning victories over the Germans), and so it was — for a few months, until everybody forgot about the change and reverted to using October. Over the years, the following names were also imposed on October, none to last: the emperor Antonius; Faustina, his wife; and Hercules.

October signaled the end of military operations in the Roman world. At this time, the Roman army honored the god Mars with a sacrifice. First, the entire army gathered on the wide Field of Mars that lay just beyond Rome's walls. Centurions then led a snow-white mount through the silent ranks of the army, until the poor beast, no doubt trembling, stood alone and innocent in the midst of the greatest fighting force on earth. A few savage blows quickly dispatched the "October Horse": a final gift from brutal men to the most brutal of gods.

In the north, the Angles called October Wyn-monath, "wine month"; the vintage for the rest of the year was pressed at this time. The Germans named it Winterfyllith, meaning "winter now is full," because the first full moon of the month signaled the onset of winter. More moon lore grew around this time of year in the

New World. The first full moon after the vernal equinox, which sometimes rises in September but more often glows above the early night skies of October, was called the hunter's moon by Indians and settlers alike. Under the bright "luminary clock against the sky," hunting bands could stalk their prey through the night, shooting more game for the coming winter.

October is the antipode of April. Just as the earth opens gloriously in the early days of spring, so does she close gloriously in the infancy of winter. October brings hyacinth dying into autumn leaf, cerulean skies, and, toward the end of the day, private fires being stoked. Diamond-sharp stars rise early, draping the evenings in a spangled mantle. Sudden squadrons of retreating geese, calling farewell to the hunter's moon, haunt the nights. October bears wood smoke, and other dark scents: dried apple and Indian corn, bonfire and scorched pumpkin. In October, nature surrenders herself to death with a magnanimity that shames her observers into recalling the brevity of life's gift. During the shortening days and splendid nights of this loveliest of months, we recall the past, the bitter and the sweet. Old loves are remembered, and other fallen summers, and spirits are glimpsed at the verge of the flaming wood.

October 31–November 2

Cross-Quarter Day

Samhain, Halloween, All Saints' Day

Let the blue wind blow toward Halloween
The night when dead souls are satisfied,
Furies hidden, angers masked and unseen
Figures walk in shadow. Those who lied,
Betrayed, bewitched, bewildered, are forgiven.
You to me and me to you: all sins shriven.

— Joseph R. Judge
"Pavane for a Dead Princess"

Halloween is a genuine pagan survivor — perhaps the only one we've really got left — virtually unchanged in character and purpose since the Celts howled on the moors under a different north star.

Every year, on October 31, America becomes a part of the ancient world. Halloween predates Christianity by at least five hundred years and is probably more venerable than that, surviving virtually intact from the earliest days of Europe. Halloween is, simply, the oldest continually celebrated festival in the Western world.

Other festivals with lineages as old mark the calendar — Christmas, Easter, New Year's — but unlike Halloween, they have undergone dramatic changes. New Year's Eve, once celebrated at the vernal equinox, is now celebrated in midwinter. Christmas and Easter, once pagan celestial festivals, have been transformed into Christian feasts. Only Halloween has remained resolutely pagan in character and content; not even the date of its celebration has changed.

During the observance of Halloween, we partake in the life of our ancestors. For they, too, entered into the spirit of this night; they, too, told ghost stories, dressed in costumes, cracked nuts by roaring bonfires, read fortunes, feared magic, saluted the dead.

The great Celtic New Year festival of Samhain began at the setting of the sun on October 31 and continued through the night until the first pale dawn of November. At Samhain the cattle were driven in from their pastures and stabled for the cold months ahead. The harvest was brought up from the earth and bundled away in cellars to sustain the community until the dawn of another spring. For the Celts, Samhain was the hinge of the year, partaking equally in the dual mysteries of life and death. On the one hand, they celebrated the bounties of the harvest, the gifts of the earth; on the other, they recognized the coming of winter, the whistling cold beyond the wattle, the chill gray dying of the world.

All of the world's nights were contained in this one night. The Celts called it "the first night of a year measured in nights," and regarded it as a living example of eternity. The great Celtic scholars Alwyn and Brinely Reese note, "At Halloween the elimination of boundaries, between the dead and living, between the sexes, between one man's property and another's and, in divinations, between the present and the future, all symbolize the return of chaos. This day partakes of the nature of eternity."

In pagan Ireland, Samhain began with a ceremony that reenacted the creation of the world by the primordial gods. Just before twilight, people all over the island extinguished their hearth fires. After the fall of night, the druids assembled on the hill of Tara, the symbolic heart of the country. There they kindled a new fire with sacred oak. From this fire, all of the hearths of the nation were relit.

Fire served another, more grisly purpose. Although animal sacrifices were the norm in Celtic ceremonies, at times of disaster, or during great festivals like Samhain, the Celts sought the favor of the gods by offering up the most potent gift they could image — human life.

The ceremony, as described by Caesar and other ancient writers, was the stuff of nightmare. Men and women, young and old, criminals and innocents, were forced into huge wood and thatch cages. Often these cages were fashioned into the shape of giants — "wicker men." Along with the human victims, goats, chickens, cats, and other animals were crowded into the great frames, along with wine, honey, and bread. At a signal from the presiding druids, these immense structures were torched, every shrieking, bleating, cackling, mewing thing in them burned to cinders.

Horses were also sacrificed. They represented Bel, the sun god, who would win back the world in the spring. After the sacrifices, great feasts were held, during which the stores of fruit and dried beef prepared during harvest were opened for the first time.

These thanksgiving feasts were held around roaring bonfires set on hillsides throughout Celtic Europe. The fires brought the new year's festival to an apex. Kindled in honor of the dwindling sun, they were thought to lend him strength during his winter exile. The tradition of these "need fires" lasted in Celtic countries until the twentieth century; in Scotland they were called the Samhagen lights — an echo of the old sacred name. Travelers lucky enough to have seen them recorded their breathtaking beauty: islands of flashing lights, visible for miles around, burning against the immense October darkness.

Samhain had a dual purpose, reflecting both fear and honor for the dead. On this night, which contained

A Celtic "wicker man," in which sacrificial victims were burned.

all nights, all times, the wall between the worlds was very thin indeed; to roam out-of-doors after dusk could prove fatal. The Celts believed that those who had died in a state of sin during the previous year had been transformed into animals as part of their penance. Now they were called back to the earth for judgment. The gods decided whether they would remain in animal shape for another year or be released into paradise. Called forth to trial, the spirits of the dead hovered all around; if angry at their purgatorial state, they could do great mischief. The power of evil sorcerers was also at its fullest, and the fairy folk were out in force and bent on wicked tricks.

For all of its supernatural perils, Samhain was a time of celebration and renewal, a time to comfort spirits in pain. Room was made around the fire for wandering souls to come and warm themselves; food and drink were laid out in offering. Ghosts were welcomed in from the darkness and offered a bit of barley cake and a cup of wine. In his magnificent poem "All Souls' Night," W. B. Yeats reiterates the age-old custom:

> Midnight has come, and the great Christ Church Bell
> And many a lesser bell chime through the room;
> And it is All Soul's Night.
> And two long glasses brimmed with muscatel
> Bubble upon the table. A ghost may come;
> For it is a ghost's right,

His element is so fine
Being sharpened by his death,
To drink from the wine-breath
While our gross palates drink from the whole wine.

To further welcome the dead, the Celts dressed as animals. Wearing shaggy skins with horns tied around their heads, they danced and sang through the night. As the dawn rose, they made a great parade to the edge of the settlement, leading the ghosts into paradise. The living comforted the dead in the face of a common fate. With the first of November came the New Year, and the cycle began again.

And so from the Celts we receive Halloween's supernatural splendors, the conviction that the Other Side presses very close, the prevalence of fairies and spirits, costumes and mischief. Children all over America act out reduced versions of the old Celtic rituals — from neighborhood bonfires to the threatened pranks of restless little spirits. Even the traditional colors of the holiday reflect its Celtic origin: orange represents the autumn harvest, while black is, of course, the symbol of death.

For all of its frightening imagery, Halloween is a happy night, full of games and laughter. Much of this buoyancy comes from the Romans, who, although banning human sacrifice, allowed the conquered Celts to continue most of their Samhain rites. As Romans and

Halloween, illustrated in *The Delineator,* 1919.

Celts intermarried, new rites, Roman in origin, were added to the festival. Chief among them was the worship of Pomona, Roman goddess of the harvest.

Representing bounty and fecundity, Pomona was depicted in Roman art sitting on a large basket of fruits and flowers, a cornucopia at her feet. Her festival was held in early November, just after the last harvest. Apples were her sacred fruit, and many games of divination involving apples entered the Samhain celebration through her influence. One of the most popular involved bobbing for apples: a large tub was filled with water and apples, then blindfolded players took turns trying to catch the floating apples in their teeth.

Pomona softened the dreadful Celtic feast. Her festival, a happy celebration of the harvest, brought Roman games and music, burning tapers and feasting. Still, Celtic notions of the supernatural clung stubbornly to the festival through the years of Roman rule and into the triumph of the church.

The same Pope Gregory who urged his French disciples to slaughter horses at Samhain in the name of Christ also moved the feast of All Hallows', All Saints' Day, from May 13 to November 1. Grafted onto one of the church's greatest holy days, Samhain became known as All Hallows' Eve, contracted over years of casual usage to Allhallows' E'en, and, ultimately, Halloween.

These early medieval centuries began the slow transformation of Halloween from a religious observance into a folk tradition. The religion of druidism that had supported the original ritual was destroyed, first by Romans and then by Christian priests. Parades were still held through the country villages, but increasingly only children went about in costume, not to appease ancestral spirits but to frighten their neighbors into parting with a few sweets. Dressed as beings from the new mythology of Christendom — saints and angels, witches and devils — they promised with a song to pray for people's souls in exchange for a "soul cake":

Soul! Soul! For a soul cake;
Pray, good mistress, for a soul cake.
An apple, a pear, a plum, a cherry,
Any good thing to make us all merry.
One for Peter, two for Paul,
Three for them that made us all.
Up with the kettle and down with your pan;
Give me a good one, and I'll be gone.

Note the concealed threat of the last line. If the cake was not forthcoming, you might find your windows broken or your butter churn emptied on the stoop. The old belief in malicious fairies and elves roaming the night was slowly evolving into the children's custom of trick-or-treat.

But as we have seen, Catholic Europe had a pagan memory. In Wales, devout Christian families still burned bonfires on Halloween, still danced and sang around them, still told ghost stories and cast fortunes by their light — and in the morning, it being All Saint's day, trooped off to church. In the Scottish Highlands the people, led by the parish priest, carried burning torches through the fields in imitation of the sun, a sure ritual to protect the fields from marauding sprites or blasting witches.

The Reformation almost killed all of this dark fancy. Reformers like Calvin, whose brittle, obsessive imagination could not conceive of anything beautiful coming from either Catholicism or its pagan antecedent, damned Halloween as a satanic observance. He claimed that the church, in allowing it and other old festivals like May Day to continue for so long, revealed itself as a diabolical institution. The threatened church launched a counterreformation, and used the Inquisition to brutally suppress any customs that smelled even remotely of magic or paganism.

Halloween rites vanished on the Continent. Even in the face of stiff persecution, however, Celtic nations like Scotland and Ireland clung stubbornly to the old ways. And in the late fifteenth century, an event occurred that ensured the survival and growth of Halloween in a land very far from its genesis. In 1492, Columbus landed in the New World.

At first, Halloween was not celebrated in America. The original Puritan settlers naturally banned it. Not until the vast Irish and Scottish immigrations of the nineteenth century did Halloween become a widespread holiday in America. Proudly Celtic, these new Americans called Halloween Oidche Shamhna, "the night of Samhain," and kept up the traditional observances. The Irish brought a particular custom with them that has become an indelible symbol of Halloween in the States — they made jack-o'-lanterns.

The original jack-o'-lanterns were potatoes or

turnips carved and illuminated by Irish children to light Halloween gatherings. They commemorated Jack, a shifty villain so wicked that neither God nor the devil would have him. Rejected by the sacred and profane, Jack wandered the world endlessly looking for a place to rest, his only light and warmth a guttering candle in a rotten gourd. In the American pumpkin — larger and easier to carve than a potato — the Irish found a grand new lantern for Jack.

America adapted and revived Halloween. Boisterous celebrations, held in barns or village squares, spread west with the young country. By the twentieth century, jack-o'-lanterns glowed on front stoops across the country. Halloween, now a night for children, its ritual origins lost and forgotten, became a fixture on the American calendar.

Halloween has overcome invasion, conversion, Inquisition, and indifference to survive and flourish in America. Despite the fact that new zealots are attacking the feast as a satanic practice, banning parades and parties in schools across the nation, old Samhain will survive and endure. Its enemies, powerful though they may be, lack the imagination to understand that they might just as well issue proclamations against the turning of the autumn leaves; the season and its great festival are linked together in the imaginative life of the West.

Besides, Halloween still has lessons to teach us, children that we are of a fractured age. It reminds us that although we can behold eternity in the dark vault of the sky, we are not eternal. In embracing death and the monsters of the night, Halloween commands us to build a common fire during a communal harvest, to pause in our hurry; to mark with joy the passing of the seasons; to glory in the ineluctable passage of time. We wrap ourselves in sheets and walk as ghosts because we know that we will, at the end of our journeys, become ghosts; and we welcome to the fire those hovering souls who whisper with our own voices.

And they still come forth. Harder to see or to sense, perhaps; but they still come forth. So this year, on the great wild night when all sins are forgiven, all souls satisfied and all creatures of the dark made welcome, be aware. They still, in spite of electric light and cynicism, hover keening in the air. This year, if you are walking down some festive street amid the throng, and you see a figure coming toward you wrapped in a black cloak, hefting a long scythe and wearing a greasepaint skull, beware. Do not tug on his cloak or try to steal his weapon, or reach out to smudge his makeup. He, in his turn, is obeying an impulse toward ritual as old as the race; you, as his observer, are gazing upon one of the faces of God.

November

The Beauty of the Bone

The sheep fairs had been held. The plums had tumbled off the trees in the first big winds, and here and there, in the lovely sunlight too soon enfee-bled, a branch of beech or oak was turning yellow: the one to die quickly and mercifully, the other perhaps to hold grimly to the frozen tree and to hiss with its papery skeletons all through the east winds of winter, until spring was there again.

— T. H. White
The Sword in the Stone

ursuing the Pleiades, Orion looms up in the east; winter's hunter returns amid shortening days and chill nights. Pegasus now dominates the southern sky; his wings beat the late-autumn winds into life, bringing an end to the harvest and the onset of cold days. The stars and the stories they tell prepare us to close one celestial year and begin another. Orion will soon return to rule for a time, but will flee with the rumor of Scorpio. The summer triangle will drop away south, but invariably return next April. Life is small, brief, and uncertain, but the ineluctable life of the lights in the night sky continues beyond human will or hope. In November, constellations not seen for months return to remind us, in the midst of a dying season, of the beautiful certainty of our small corner of the infinite night.

The Roman senate attempted to name November after the emperor Tiberius, whose birthday fell in November. He refused the honor, reminding the Senate that they had already renamed two of the year's twelve months after members of his family, and finally sneering, "What shall you do, conscript fathers, if you find yourself with thirteen Caesars?"

To the Saxons, November was Midmonath, "month of strong winds"; they also called it Blotmonath, literally, "blood month." Cattle and pigs were slaughtered, their flesh to be jerked or smoked to provide winter larders with meat.

Before the weather turns for the last time, an occasional gift arrives in the form of a few days — or a week or more — of warm, even hazy weather. In Europe, this mild reprieve became known as Saint Martin's summer, because it usually came around November 11, the saint's feast day. In America, the same spell of mild weather was called Indian summer.

Explanations for the origin of this phrase vary. Some etymologists claim that it comes from the fact that settlers across the Alleghenies noticed that summer seemed to last longer in the sheltered valleys of the western or "Indian" lands — Kentucky, Tennessee, and the low wide valley of the Mississippi — than they did on the brittle East Coast. A more popular, romantic explanation claims that at this final warm time of the year, the natives could gather together for one last big hunt before the straying game herds finally headed south.

A time of gathering quiet and early snow, November carries us into winter. Green leaf fades to brown, which crumbles from naked twig. Below baring branches, earth's floor grows thick with orphaned children. Above, the cerulean blue of the sky envelopes the dark sycamore branch, offering a glimpse of cold immortality — but not for us.

Deer bed down deep in the thinning November forests, wary of men with loud guns. They move fitfully between the trees, and start up at the smallest rustle on the forest floor. When they feel secure enough to venture from the depths of the woods, they graze in backyards or open fields. To see a family of whitetails facing into a stiff November wind is to become reacquainted with the sanctity of life's quiet autumn struggle. Slanting November light catches their antlers and ripples along their flanks. For a moment, they look to be the Elgin marbles sprung to life, and gray November becomes the most beautiful of seasons.

Thanksgiving

At the evening meal there was less form and circumstance; and when the winter night closed in, when the flame crackled and the sparks streamed up the wide-throated chimney, the founders of New France gathered around the blaze. Then did the Grand Master resign the collar to the successor of his honors, and, with jovial courtesy, pledge him in a cup of wine. Thus did these ingenious Frenchmen beguile the winter of their exile.

— Francis Parkman
France and England in North America

 ometimes, through chance or determination, an all-but-extinct custom is rediscovered and restored to life. We have seen how America breathed new life into Halloween. Thanksgiving, following close behind the old Celtic festival, is another ancient practice resurrected in the New World. Those responsible were not ethnic immigrants consciously restoring the traditions of their ancestors. They were a small group of Puritan settlers, mostly English and Dutch, who wanted to leave everything about Europe — its Catholicism, customs, and political systems — far behind.

The Pilgrims (as they called themselves and as we remember them) who established the second English colony in America had been persecuted for decades by just about everybody: by the short-lived Catholic hierarchy in England; by Charles I, the king fated to have his head knocked off by Oliver Cromwell; by their fellow Protestants, who thought they went too far in their ideas about communal living. During the early years of the seventeenth century, Cromwell's ascendancy lay some decades away, and the Puritans found their backs against the wall. They practiced an unwavering version of Protestantism, as strict as it was heartfelt and sincere — a dangerous element in the culture war enveloping England. Church and state persecuted them alike. In 1619, the church members decided that they would only find true religious freedom by decamping from England and Europe altogether. They had a few friends among the nobility; a deal was brokered with the crown whereby they would be granted lands in the New World in exchange for leaving their homelands forever.

In the fall of 1620, after a cramped and dreadful voyage across the Atlantic on a tiny ship called the *Mayflower*, the small band of outcasts made landfall at Cape Cod. They brought with them a printing press (they had actually used it to stabilize one of the ship's cracked beams during a storm), several cows, a deep love of their God and their freedom, and a myopic, un-yielding, but by the standards of their brutal time liberated vision of how the world worked.

The Pilgrims were a study in contradiction. They were perhaps the most sincere human beings who ever lived. They believed that the heathen shores of America could be transformed into God's living kingdom on earth, and within hours after touching down (a space-age term, but it applies to them, literally landing as they did on a new world), they began their work. They elected their leaders, called elders, the undisputed authorities in the colony. They established a social code both rigid and practical. All would attend prayers, as a community, every day. Wives could not disagree with the judgments of their husbands. All would hunt for a communal pot, and a man could take a refreshing drink at a "Necessary" — their fitting term for a tavern. Festivals being forms of papist idolatry, Christmas and Easter observances were outlawed. The Indians were to be either converted or, failing that, exterminated.

The Pilgrims probably believed in the recently published propaganda of John Smith, who had transformed the hell of the Jamestown colony into a rip-roaring yarn of adventure west beyond the neap tide: the vast Chesapeake, leaping with fish and pregnant with oyster and crab; lovely, lithe Pocahontas; drums in the twilight. A lost, exciting Eden to be populated by the faithful.

*   *   *

Their first winter dispelled such notions. They came from temperate England, where even in winter the temperature rarely drops below freezing. Now they tried to survive, with only will and a few starving cows, a savage Massachusetts winter. November brought freezing rains and endless winds; and after that came the snow. It did not stop falling until April. The northeast wind, frozen into steel by the offshore Labrador Current, blew with enough strength to knock a man dead in his tracks. It did that to many.

The colony barely survived that first winter; by spring, little more than half of the original settlers were still alive. But they were alive. They had made it through the blasting icy cold, and when spring came, they began to work in the welcome sun.

The following fall saw a hardy little colony growing on the Massachusetts Bay. Governor John Bradford thought that the pilgrims should mark their first anniversary in the New World with a feast of prayer and thanksgiving. In a proclamation, he set December 13, 1621, as the date upon which the colonists should express their gratitude to Almighty God for "the bounties we have received in the new land of hardship and struggle."

On the morning of the thirteenth, a rare mild one, Bradford told the four best shots in the settlement to head for the woods and shoot enough game for a feast. The men went off to hunt while the rest of the settlement crowded into the rough little wooden church for the first recorded Thanksgiving service held on the soil of North America.

The service probably lasted all day. Continental Puritans went to church at sunup and remained sequestered in their pews until late in the afternoon, and there is no reason to suppose that the pilgrims relaxed the requirements of piety, even in the face of the brooding wild.

At some point afterward, the marksmen returned. Their efforts exceeded all expectations: a passel of quail, a few pheasant, and four or five enormous turkeys. The women immediately began to pluck the birds, while the men prepared the fires and the spits.

Some ninety Indians soon arrived, attracted no doubt by the scent of roasting fowl. Their chief, Massasoit, after whom that whole land would later be named, led them. They came not to steal or to make war but to share, presenting the nervous colonists with five deer. Bradford, grateful, relieved, invited the "children of the forest" to join the feast. It lasted five days, after which whites and Indians pledged oaths of mutual peace and brotherhood. In the chilly dawn of the early New England winter, with the game eaten and the fires dying, the Indians sang a last song to the Pilgrims. This song, undoubtedly improvised for the occasion, probably concerned brotherhood and good wishes for the people facing the hard winter coming. After they had finished their song, the Indians gathered up some food and drifted off into the thinning woodlands, unaware that they had been singing a hymn to their own eventual destruction.

As the years went by, Thanksgiving days were proclaimed in the colonies as circumstances dictated. If a fine harvest had been gathered, the governor of this or that colony would proclaim a day of Thanksgiving. A national day of this sort did not begin to take shape until the Revolution, when no less than eight days of national thanks were proclaimed by the Continental Congress to celebrate major victories against the British.

The first move to celebrate a national day of thanksgiving did not come about until 1789, when George Washington tried to set November 26 as a nationwide day of rest, prayer, and thanks. Differences of culture and politics between the new states soon made Washington's edict fade away, and another Thanksgiving was not widely celebrated in the United States until the Civil War, when Abraham Lincoln called for one after the Union's defensive victory at Antietam.

Although Lincoln's declaration was only meant for wartime, a determined and enterprising woman, Sarah Hale, editor of the very popular magazine *Godey's Lady's Book,* used her influence to lobby for an official national Thanksgiving holiday. She convinced Lincoln, and in 1864 he officially named the last Thursday in November Thanksgiving Day.

*   *   *

At Thanksgiving, we celebrate the simple fact of our continued existence, and we do it simply. There are no elaborate national or religious ceremonies on this day. Each family, in its own way, performs rituals of its own device. Some play football in the morning, watch the famous parade on television, sneak a taste of turkey from the roasting bird. The casualness of the holiday, its simplicity, emulates neither the high drama of Christmas nor the eerie theatricality of Halloween, but contents itself with small and simple acts that reinforce the mere joy of being alive. We pray, we drink, and we eat. At the end of the day, as uncles doze in front of late games, folks sneak out back to smoke, dishes are gathered up and washed with ceremony, and the dusk falls, the grayness of the early winter night makes the fire in the grate seem brighter, and the chill in the air makes the house seem warmer. The trees, robbed of their leaves, display the loveliness of a world stripped to its simple essence; a hard world, but beautiful. Thanksgiving is only what it claims to be about: giving thanks that we are all together, in hope.

Children have an even better reason to enjoy the day. They look into the deepening night and smile, knowing that just around the corner, the lights of Christmas wait.

December

The Invincible Sun

The pitchy gloom without makes the heart dilate on entering the room filled with the glow and warmth of the evening fire. The ruddy blaze diffuses an artificial summer and sunshine through the room, and lights up each countenance in a kindlier welcome. Where does the honest face of hospitality expand into a broader and more cordial smile — where is the shy glance of love more sweetly eloquent — than by the winter fireside? And as the hollow blast of wintry wind rushes through the hall, claps the distant door, whistles about the casement, and rumbles down the chimney, what can be more grateful than that feeling of sober and sheltered security with which we look around upon the comfortable chamber and the scene of domestic hilarity?

— Washington Irving
"Christmas"

tep outside on a December morning and remember June: sprinklers hissing, the ululating buzz of insects, birdsong chiming against the dense, humid air. Life's song, the song of the sun; energy translated into leaf, bowel, heart, muscle, and throat from a furnace blazing 29 million miles away. Now consider the December that surrounds you. The sun dwells far in the south, and the daytime world is cold, quiet, brooding. No insects chime or buzz; grass sleeps matted under leaf or snow; summer's birds have flown away. The night sky also announces winter's triumph: Cygnus dives into the southern sea, seeking warmer climes below the equator; Orion raises his great bow in triumph; the great Bear cleaves the land with her frosty claws.

December might literally mean "ten" — Roman insistence on order again — but despite its prosaic name, it is the richest and most imaginative of months. December closes and awakens the year: it brings darkness, and great light. It kills the world, and resurrects it. It slays the sun, and leads the way to summer.

The ritual year begins during December, when, at the winter solstice, the sun reaches its most distant point in the southern sky. The shortest day of the year commences. Dawn comes late, and the sun sets early. Darkness surrounds pale light. Our ancestors answered the question of what to do when the sun seemed lost by making the season a holy celebration of life.

If it is to complete its long journey home, the sun now needs the aid of high hearts and hillside fires, of glasses raised in fellowship, of hushed holy vigils. Even now, when the fire of life seems so far away, so helpless in the grip of winter, we notice, if we watch the sky with the attention and wonder of our ancestors, that the journey back from the void has already begun. Imperceptible to all but the most patient eyes, the days henceforth will expand, stealing back a little light from the darkness with each turn of the earth.

To celebrate this promised return, we create small suns of our own. Candles illuminate windows, and evergreen trees stand in our family rooms; living altars are draped with light, defiantly illuminating the deepening gloom. Rituals of renewal and rebirth crowd this dark time, as they have from the beginning of recorded history, and will continue until the dawn of spring and nature's reawakening at Easter.

The magic works, every time. As January melts into February, that same small flicker of the sun will grow, swell, get hotter and closer, until the warming days and pleasant tasks of spring remind us that, on some level of reality beyond the grasp of mortal mind, not even death lasts forever. Only then, with the world secure in the grip of summer, does the calendar relax its vigil over the planets, the stars, the sun, the moon, the winds, the breezes, the gates of dawn, and the ramparts of night. In December, when the early darkness falls, humanity wills strength and summer back into the world.

Step outside on a December evening and see the birth of June. Down the street, colored lights, strung across boxwoods or evergreens or along the aluminum lines of rain gutters, shine into the gelid air. Listen. Singers raise carols to the faraway stars. They are singing to a babe. They are also singing to the sun.

Advent

From the Sunday nearest
Saint Andrew's Day to Christmas

O come O dayspring from on high
And cheer us by your drawing nigh.
Dispense the gloomy clouds of night
And death's dark shadow put to flight.
Rejoice! Rejoice! Emmanuel
Shall come to thee, O Israel!

— "O Come, O Come, Emmanuel"

The word itself comes from the Latin, an old conjoining of two simple words. *Ad*, "to," and *venire*, "to come." Literally, to come to. Advent, then, is the time of preparation for Christmas, recognized by the Roman, Greek, Lutheran, and Anglican churches. It is a joyful Lent — like Lent, it lasts for forty days; unlike Lent, it prepares us not for a death but for a birth.

The earliest record of something like Advent being observed is found in a canon from the council of Saragossa, held in A.D. 380, which forbids anyone to be absent from church services from December 17 (the same date on which the Roman Saturnalia began) to the Epiphany.

Sony:

Vito Del Deo /

input

① D.V. input—
   IEEE 1394
   Firewire

② soft way: ↗
   ⓐ Aboabe Premi
   ⓑ Avid
   ⓒ Pinnical
   ⓓ digital oragins

addon:
DVD recorder.

In the fifth century, Advent became even more severe, as a Lent-type fast of forty days, from Martinmas (November 11) to Christmas Eve. Later this period was shortened, until by the ninth century Advent took on the schedule it still has today: from the Sunday nearest the feast of Saint Andrew (November 30) to Christmas.

The old strictures that made Advent an austere time have virtually disappeared; it is now a happy season, full of parties and presents, Christmas carols and revelry; a time when you get a belly full of eggnog, warm your tail at the fire, give your love a roll, and in spite of life's trials count your blessings.

But a few reminders of Advent's severe past are still around: Fridays are fast days; the church organ can't play until the third week of Advent (when it announces the Savior's imminence); and the priests wear the purple of penance all season, except on the feasts of the saints. Also, among old-timers it is still considered very unlucky to marry during the Advent season.

Many lovely Advent customs have sadly vanished. In Normandy farmers used to pick a night in Advent to send their little children running through the fields, carrying flaming brands and singing songs to drive the pests away:

> Mice and moles get out of my field!
> I will burn your beard and bones!
> Trees and shrubs, give me bushels of apples!

Okay, that's not so lovely. But it is fascinating. The children obviously represented the Christ child, come to earth to drive all the evil away. Imitative magic is at work — "As the Christ Child drove away sin, so do these children drive away vermin." It's also interesting to note that no girl over twelve could participate. Menstruation spoiled the magic — yet another example of paganism and Catholicism combining without really knowing it.

Now this *is* lovely: in Rome, during the final days of Advent, the Calabrian *pifferari*, or bagpipe players, enter the city and pass by every shrine, saluting the Virgin Mary with their trilling, wild music. Their intention is to soothe her in the growing pains of her holy labor. The Italians believe that the bagpipe — an ancient instrument — was the favorite instrument of the Virgin, and that the original shepherds who came to worship at the feet of baby Jesus played their bagpipes for him. The *pifferari* also stop at carpenter shops, out of respect for Saint Joseph. I do not know whether the Romans still play for the Madonna; let's hope they do.

The most popular living Advent custom is of course caroling, although in this sad and dangerous age you hear more of it in shopping malls than you do on the streets, or before your threshold. Still, the music is lovely, and reminds us that somewhere in the East a bright star once shone.

December 17–25

Quarter Day

Winter Solstice, Yule, Christmas

Some say that ever 'gainst that season comes
Wherein our savior's birth is celebrated
The bird of dawning singeth all night long.
And then, they say, no spirit dares stir abroad;
The nights are wholesome; and then no planets strike,
No fairy takes nor witch hath power to charm,
So hallowed and so gracious is the time.

— William Shakespeare
Hamlet

Christmas is the most anticipated and widely observed festival in the world. Even non-Christian countries celebrate the season: in Japan, giving gifts at this time has become a new tradition, and the Chinese honor Santa Claus under the sobriquet of "Christmas Old Man." In the waning days of December, people across the globe sing carols and decorate their homes, exchange presents

under Christmas trees, and hold candlelit vigils to prepare human hearts for the birth of the Christian savior.

Of course many saviors have appeared to many
cultures throughout the millennia, and people living
above the equator have used the winter solstice to
honor those saviors since the start of recorded history.
Since for so many ancient civilizations the sun embodied divinity, the day on which our star began to return
north naturally became one of the chief holy days of
the year. And unlike other holy days, solstice time became a cause for great celebration and joy, a party held
in the face of earth's darkest hour. The celebrations, in
fact, usually lasted for more than a week, the actual day
of the solstice falling midway through the festival.

The Romans certainly enjoyed themselves at the
close of December, as did their ferocious neighbors to
the north, Celt and German alike. Bits and pieces of many
solstice observances, from myriad cultures, all found
their way into the modern celebration of Christmas.
And they were the same that produced our calendar
(the calendar and its festive children walk, after all,
hand in hand): Roman, Celtic, and German. And so we
find ourselves at the perfect close of our journey through
the year.

The gregarious and festive tones of Christmas, the
tradition of spending December evenings drinking,
flirting, and dancing the night away, come from the Roman Saturnalia. Its darker hues, which Charles Dickens

used to such brilliant effect in *A Christmas Carol,* are legacies of the ancient Germans and their wild, almost sinister observance of Yule.

In temperate Rome, the farmers gathered their final harvests during the middle of December, and afterward the city threw one last party before the dark, ghostly days of winter. The Romans called it the Saturnalia, and aspects of the great feast still vividly live on in modern Christmas celebrations.

The Romans thought that the world had known three ages. The first had been the age of Saturn, the

The Roman Saturnalia.

oldest of the gods, and the kindest. During the bliss of his reign, called the Golden Age, man and woman walked naked together on an earth that knew no winter. Fruit dropped from every tree, the lion and the lamb slept as brother and sister, and war was unknown. Saturn, thrown out of heaven by the upstart Jupiter, wandered off into lonely exile. With his departure, the world began to lose its sheen, and each succeeding age — the Silver and the Iron — proved more miserable than the last. Every year, beginning on December 17 and continuing for eight days, the Romans attempted to bring a bit of Saturn's golden age back in the Saturnalia, a festival of guiltless, unbridled debauchery.

Unlike old Saturn's innocent age, the Saturnalia was little more than a citywide orgy. The poet Sallust reports that, "Most people went naked to parties and even through the streets. Absolute license reigned. Drinking was constant. Servants and their masters switched places, with the lord of the house feasting his slaves and the lady of the house washing the feet of her maids."

This was, to say the least, a carefree time. The Romans were as sensual as they were hardworking, and they have bequeathed us the notion that, as holy as it may be, the solstice allows poor mortals a degree of license. It was this quality of the celebration that would later so offend the Puritans, who went so far as to outlaw the celebration altogether, claiming, correctly, that it was simply an excuse for the common people to overdrink and collapse into bed with one another. Yet despite their efforts, the season still extends its invitation to misbehave, as bleary survivors of modern Christmas parties can testify.

As Rome conquered Europe, aspects of the Saturnalia grafted themselves onto local customs, not least the ribald customs of the feast. The mistletoe, hung throughout Celtic Europe in December as a symbol of eternal life, became an invitation for sexual contact: hung above lintels and from door frames, or the central rafter of the hall, it invited any who stood beneath to share a lingering kiss.

Rome's weeklong party had its genteel side. Romans sent one another small gifts, wrapped in papyrus or oilskin, and held open houses during which passersby were invited to come in and enjoy cakes and mulled wine. These simple acts of civic gentility bound the community together in the face of encroaching winter. And they still do. Christmas gifts and welcoming homes hearken back to the happy Roman riot of the Saturnalia, during which an otherwise militant people laid down their swords and created a fleeting world of love, sensual delight, neighborly kindness, and good cheer — and during which any intelligent enemy could surely have conquered the place.

The introduction of the Christ child into the Saturnalia happened during the fifth century A.D., when the church transferred the observance of the Savior's birth from its traditional date in spring to December 25.

The switch made political sense; Christian leaders wanted their greatest feast day associated with a venerable Roman celebration. Members of the early church were recruited from the pagan population, and the establishment of a festival at this time could focus the attention of the converted on a Christian festival. But the church leaders had another, very pressing concern that made them switch the holiday. Throughout the fifth century, the young faith ferociously competed with a rival sect that for a time threatened the very existence of Christianity: the cult of Mithras.

Mithras was a Persian god of light whose chief symbol was the sun. He promised eternal life to the brave, and became a favorite of Roman soldiers garrisoned in the Levant. When the soldiers returned home to Rome, they brought Mithras with them. His worshippers celebrated his birthday on December 25, which they called *natalis invicti solis*, "the birth of the unconquerable sun." Thanks to the soldiers, and because the feast of Mithras was entwined with the pleasures of the Saturnalia, it soared in popularity, and the sect eventually became a serious rival to the early church.

Faced with stiff competition from an upstart god of the East, the followers of another upstart god of the East decided to embark on a bit of public relations. They declared publicly that not Mithras but Christ had been born on December 25, and that the followers of Mithras were only aping the birth of the true Son of God.

This canny bit of propaganda did not sit well with some early church leaders, who claimed that it smacked of sun worship, paganism, and idolatry. They were right, of course; but in the end, the more politically acute bishops won out, and the day of the Lord's birth was officially switched from the spring to December.

Christmas (literally, "the mass of Christ") was a roaring success from the start. It combined the fine old debauchery of the Saturnalia with the genuine piety of the church to create the perfect holiday: one in which you could misbehave and feel holy at the same time. Drink and prayer, feasting and caring for the poor; they all walked hand in hand through the season. Even after the fall of the empire, the traditions culled from both pagan and Christian, from Saturnalia and sacred manger, continued to be observed by people throughout Europe.

The next addition to the Christmas story came during the early Middle Ages, as decrepit Rome gave way to the new barbarian kingdoms, and Germanic peoples grafted their own customs onto the feast.

Long before the name of Christ appeared in Europe, the Germans celebrated the end of December as the dawn of their year. They called it Yule, a word still used by people everywhere as a synonym for Christmas.

The word is most probably Gothic in origin. The

Goths, a particularly vivid and imaginative branch of the German family, called their December festival and the potent ale they drank during it (in prodigious quantities) by the same name: *oel*, pronounced "yule." This word is cognate with their word *hiul*, meaning, simply, "wheel." This linkage makes lovely sense: the image of the wheel gave the Goths a symbolic image of both the sun and its wheeling trip through the seasons, which reached its farthest point away from them at the winter solstice. Yule was meant to help the sun turn its wheeling course around again.

During Yule the Germans (along with their northern neighbors the Celts) paid homage to the returning sun in high barbaric style. They rode out to boar hunts and roasted their prey whole over a single burning log set in the midst of the mead hall. This log, usually the trunk of a sacred oak tree, symbolized the sun's return. After the Saxon conquest of England (the Saxons and the Goths were very closely related, and shared many of the same customs), the Yule log came to Britain. Centuries later, it came with the English settlers of America across the Atlantic. Today, in taverns and great homes throughout America and Europe, people still burn the sacred Yule log at Christmas.

The season's most cherished rites fell not on Yule itself, but on its eve. It was then that, just before the return of the sun, the forces of darkness and death gathered their fullest strength. Trolls and ogres roamed the black forests; to wander outside was to invite death. Nature, so green and welcoming just months before, had become cold, dark, and terrifying. On this night the German gods, led by Odin, rode forth through the skies, rattling the heavens with their wild hunt.

The forces of light and life had now to be called back into the world, and the ancient Germans responded to this need by transforming a night of dread into one of celebration. On Yule Eve, they practiced rituals of fertility, held elaborate feasts, toasted Odin above, who protected the sun, and convinced themselves that their song and laughter in the face of darkness could influence the whole vast universe.

In the far north, the Norse offered their prayers and sacrifices to Frey, the god of fertility. They strung holly, the symbol of stubborn life, through their lodges, and draped branches of evergreen above the doors and over the beds. They drank potent ale, sang songs, and told stories before enormous fires. Late at night, men and women fell into bed together and made sleepy love in rooms scented with strung balsam, the fire casting a surety of light against the darkness behind the wattle walls.

By the high Middle Ages, Christmas had become an alleviation of winter's gray trudge; a festival of light, warmth, spirit, and food, celebrated by noble and peasant alike. It combined, with neither friction nor rancor, the pagan memories of the people and the glories of the

Christian faith. In spite of the wild revelry of Christmastime, people recognized the central point of the whole affair. They did so when they heard the tale of the child in swaddling clothes lying in a manger far off and long ago: the loving will of God translated into susceptible flesh beneath an eastern star. Freezing shepherds could wander into the castle's main hall for the feast on Christmas Eve, look at their lord at his elevated table, and know that, in spite of all the earthly power he held, their kind had been the first to find the babe; the kings came later. And so, for medieval people, commoner and royal alike, the season offered a vision of a world made one, where all would sit at a common table, in the blazing light of the Lord's mercy, and never know the cold again.

Centuries later, the rise of the Puritans threatened the very existence of Christmas. They saw the sensual cheer of the season as unacceptably pagan. In 1643 the English Parliament, controlled by Oliver Cromwell, forbade the observance of Christmas, "any law, statute, custom, constitution, or cannon to the contrary notwithstanding." For twelve dreary years, Christmas passed in England without music or dance, drink or feast.

In 1660 Charles II gained the throne. Witty, debauched, and tolerant, he restored not only the monarchy but also dicing, dancing, drinking, dalliance, the theater, and Christmas.

*   *   *

The *Mayflower* carried the anti-Christmas sentiment of the Puritans with it across the Atlantic, so the holiday took a long time to take hold in the New World. In 1659 the general court of Massachusetts ordered a Christmas ban: "Anyone found observing the abstinence from labor, feasting, or in any way any such day as Christmas day, shall be fined five shillings." The ordinance was repealed in 1668, probably because the other colonies, all enjoying the roaring times of Yule, made the people of Massachusetts feel like a collection of backward prudes.

As the years went by, and those other colonies filled with immigrants from Ireland, Scotland, and Germany, they celebrated Christmas with the tools of their ancestors: Yule logs, dances, mistletoe kisses. They also celebrated most Christmas customs not on the feast day itself, but on the night before. As we have seen, northern European peoples observed the eves of their holy days with greater passion than they did the days themselves; they transmitted their love of "the night before" to the American sensibility. Christmas Eve gradually became the true sacred time, when the world turned toward darkness for one last long night, during which something sacred and mysterious would occur while mortals slept. By the dawn of Christmas Day, the great deed — the birth of the Christ child — was considered to have been accomplished.

*   *   *

Many customs of Christmas Eve, because they sprang from the popular imagination and not clerical committees, bear the delightful stamp of the antique world. Families hold elaborate dinners, attend mass, and share recollections of days gone by. Some families still wait until Christmas Eve to decorate the most famous symbol of the season, the Christmas tree.

Pagan Germans were probably responsible for the Christmas tree. During the Yule season, they would fill their lodges with evergreens: holly, mistletoe, and balsam. Even whole firs were chopped down and set in the center of the dwelling. This practice seems to have caught on in early Christian Europe, culminating in the widespread belief that the birth of Christ should be celebrated with the decoration of an illuminated fir tree.

The English never adopted the custom, thinking it very rude and very German. The marriage of Queen Victoria to the German prince Albert finally brought the venerable tree to England. During their first Christmas together, Albert displayed a Christmas tree bedecked with flaming candles and strewn with glittering baubles in the salon of the palace. Its beauty captured the imagination of the public, and it became much the fashion during Victoria's long reign to set up a tree of one's own. It was not long before the custom spread to America.

Christmas Eve is the night when the spirit of generosity adopts a human face, much as the spirit of the Christian

Odin on his eight-legged steed, Sleipnir.

god is said to have done so long ago. In the still night, under the cold stars, as ashes die in fireplaces and children sleep fitfully in their beds, the last living mythological figure of the modern world embarks on a long and loving journey.

Santa Claus is the son of many cultures, but his chief ancestor is none other than Odin, the all-father to the Norse. During the frigid nights of Yule, Odin rode through the skies on the champing Sleipnir, searching the earth below. If he saw wickedness afoot, he would drop from the skies and punish the malefactor. The good who fell under Odin's gaze were rewarded with gifts: swords that never rusted, helms that thwarted all blades, drinking horns that never emptied. The Norse copied Odin's generosity during Yule by exchanging gifts. When Christianity came, they kept up the tradition.

Gradually, under the rubric of Nicholas, a Catholic saint whose feast day fell in December, the fierce old Norse god was tamed into the kindly, bearded night rider of Christmas Eve, and Santa's physical qualities — his flowing beard, hooded robe, and wise, merry eyes — flow directly from the god of the pagan north.

Of course that is all academic; a bit of learned doggerel concerning the myth of Santa Claus. But those who know about myths know them to be anything but untrue. And so it is with Santa. Wholly remarkable, he is our last true and surviving myth: even in an age of greed and skepticism, belief in Santa is encouraged as an article of faith in the moral education of children.

Santa Claus resides in our world. He has a home, at the North Pole. Millions of children send him letters every year, which are accepted by the post office. Meteorologists report his journey through the skies on Christmas Eve. He travels on a sleigh drawn by eight (now nine) reindeer, visits worthy children, sets gifts beneath their tree, and leaves gracious notes of thanks for the cookies and milk they have left out for him. Across the world, nervous children hear his bells jingling and the hooves of reindeer stamping against the roof.

Santa Claus rules the kingdom of childhood, and the faith that children hold in him is as unshakable as Gibraltar. For a little while. There comes a day in every life when each of us forgets the wisdom of our parent's knee. A friend whispers blasphemy. At first we close our ears, not wanting the midnight ride that Odin loaned his conqueror to vanish from the winter sky. We are pressured, cajoled, finally convinced. How can he visit everyone in one night? How can he climb down all those chimneys? Only little kids believe in him anyway. To grow up, you have to say good-bye to the idea of a grandfather for the world. And so we have a moment of interrogation. We ask our parents about it, and get many answers. In the end, we realize that such a thing simply cannot be. We make Santa Claus a lie, a fable, a mere tale. We become the Puritan with his axe to the maypole, thinking that he can defeat the spring by toppling its symbol.

It may be true that we have never seen Santa Claus. We have never seen a photon, but are awash in light; never seen the breeze, but feel it tousle our hair on spring mornings. We cannot see our souls, but we know that they hold flickering all the good we bear. It is, then, useless to debate so obvious a matter as the existence of Santa with those who have neither eyes to see, nor hearts to feel.

*   *   *

The customs of the Christmas season, pagan and frivolous, whimsical and innocent, surround the central, simple image of a child's birth in a stable. The child was born in an occupied country, during a time when one man ruled much of the civilized world, when slaves were as common as automobiles are today, and when life ended early, violently, or both. The gods, always capricious, had vested the rule of the world in glittering, panoplied Rome, and she had repaid the favor by decimating civilizations, destroying her republic, and making a fat, balding scion of the house of Caesar the apotheosis of humanity. Now a boy was born into poverty, the son of a mother of questionable virtue and of a father whom many considered a cuckold. The child was destined to live a short life, to die in pain and disgrace, and ultimately to reshape the spiritual contours of the world.

The Christmas story is one of the most beautiful and poignant narratives in human history. Luke, the author of the third Gospel, which introduced the most famous elements of the tale, was a writer of enormous psychological and poetic power. Writing in the hellenized, cosmopolitan society of the second century, Luke took care to introduce Christ properly, as a divine visitor to earth, but with a difference. He would not seek the thrones of men, but attend their hearts; he would not become rich, but live and die destitute.

Luke gives us the weary couple, Joseph and Mary, forced to return to the town of Bethlehem to pay a tax. They are overtaken by night and forced to stay among the animals in a stable, where the baby Jesus is born and bundled in a manger. Off in the fields, shepherds are told of the birth by choirs of angels, and come to visit the newborn. Three magi, Persian astronomers drawn to the spot by a mysterious new star, follow them.

Luke sprinkled his narrative with fulfilled prophecies, subtle references to other child-gods born in poverty, and angelic messengers. The simplicity of the story, with its abject couple wandering through the darkness to find shelter only among the animals, is countered by its brilliant symbolism. The Savior of Man is born in a manger, and discovered by shepherds, events that presage Christ's lifetime of ministering to the poor. The arrival of the magi, bearing their famous gifts, introduces a beguiling, occult beauty into the story, simultaneously introducing the Christ child as divine being.

A Christmas legend that gained prominence long ago is sadly fading away: the belief that at the stroke of twelve on Christmas Eve, animals everywhere speak with human voices to welcome the Savior. Generations of children opened an eye at midnight, but not to spy for Santa. They imagined the animals snug in their barns, the horses in their stalls, the cats curled around the

Franklin stove, the dogs snoring in a heap. Midnight's chime brought all awake, speaking to one another in quiet tones that the child was born.

The image seems silly to those in the thrall of insidious logic, but it makes perfect mythological sense. How better for creation to honor the birth of the Savior than for the very creatures who had warmed him with their breath to welcome him with the voices of men and of angels?

Christmas, in its essence, remains, and will always remain, despite pandering businessmen and fashionable need, a quiet and cold night, redolent of sacred air. Its stars shine brighter than most nights' stars, and the musk of fir and newborn sanctity attend its carrying breezes. It waits on the wanderer, comforts the forlorn, and promises a blessed manger to the weary. It obeys nothing more or less than the dictates of the generous heart, and expects, in return, nothing less.

December 31

New Year's Eve

Wherever in the world they may be on New Year's Eve, when, helped by drink and the reminder of their bondage to time, men and women indulge their instinct of a common humanity, they join hands and sing a song of Burns.

— M. H. Abrams

It is at this crucial junction of time, suspended between one year and the next, one life and the next, that the universe re-creates itself out of chaos. The seeds of the rest of the year lie hidden beneath the snows of New Year's Day.

Perhaps the greatest expression of this sense of January as a moment of reflection on the past and the future was penned by the great Scottish poet Robert Burns, in his famous song "Auld Lang Syne," still sung around the world at the stroke of midnight on New Year's Eve. The phrase is from the Scots, and means, roughly, "old times past."

> Should auld acquaintance be forgot
> And never brought to min'? . . .
> We'll tak a cup o' kindness yet
> For auld lang Syne

Mortals forget, Burns warns us, as life drives us forward through the sea of time; lovers fade from memory, debts of the heart are forgotten, friendships fail. On this night, which, like the other significant festivals of the year, marks a divider between seasons, tallies the years, and dwindles lives, it is necessary to pause; to remember with advantages, like Shakespeare's old soldiers, the time that we have shared with our fellow creatures. We are bounded by a common sky, hounded by the same regrets, and mutually fated to the simple disaster of death. But by New Year's Eve the sun, the life of the planet and the only immortal with whom we share intimate acquaintance, has escaped his winter prison. The universe is new again.

We, with the sun, have come full circle, following the wheeling seasons through an ancient way of seeing. Our lives are brief, but they partake in the lives of others, long dead, who live again through our delight in the world they taught us to observe. Those who came before recognized a sacred connection between the universe and themselves. They bequeathed us stories of the stars that guide season into season, summoned Santa Claus to ride the frosty rims of the world, allowed April to catch the fool, let lovers lie in May with every fragrant blessing, culled the mistletoe, waited in summer's cicadic pause for the sun to turn his head.

We end where we began, at the winter solstice: the dawn of winter, the biding triumph of returning spring, the distant hope of summer, the promised return of fall. If you read these words after yet another New Year's Eve of too much drink and too much talk of nothing; if you have bleak midwinter in your soul, an incipient hangover in your head, and an unhappy other dozing in the other room; if the world's margins seem thin; if all of your fond, youthful hopes seem blasted; if it appears that the winter will never end: rejoice. You are participating in the death and resurrection of the world.

Outside, many creatures lie buried beneath the hard soil — moles and toads, mice and their old enemies the snakes, curled in mutual frozen anticipation. Their hearts beat but once a day, and their blood is as thick as rendered oil. They, too, seem lost, their hour done; but, come the breath of April, they will stir in their tiny graves, transforming them into mangers, and a million small saviors will once again appear.

They will not live forever; not even the sun will live forever. That is the way of our creation and condition; that is the way of the world. But they will live to dance awhile under the kind sun; to feel the blossoms of spring brushing by on mild evenings under starlight. They need encouragement, hope, as does the distant, returning star we call home; as does our sweet Mother Earth during this precious, dangerous time.

If you are lucky enough, then, to feel the blues of the midwinter fugue, then you are lucky enough to know that the river runs, the round world spins, dawn and lamplight, midnight, noon. Sun follows day, night, stars, and moon. The day ends, the end begins. Get up, go to the window, hurl open the sash, and despite all past sorrow or future care, sing a song of Burns.

Picture Acknowledgments

Su Song, design for a Chinese water clock, 1088 C.E. School of African and Oriental Studies, London / The Bridgeman Art Library

The sun god Shamash receiving homage from three small figures, 9th century B.C.E. Museum of Oriental Antiquities, Istanbul, Turkey. Erich Lessing / Art Resource, N.Y.

A.H. Payne, *Diana*, engraving after fresco (Parma, Italy, c. 1519) by Correggio, 19th century. New York Public Library Picture Collection

Johann Helvelius, *Orion*, from *Uranographia*, 1690. New York Public Library Picture Collection

Julian calender, Byzantine era. Museo Arcivescovile, Ravenna, Italy. Scala / Art Resource, N.Y.

Coligny Calender, Gallic lunar calender in Celtic language using Roman letters and numerals, late 1st–early 2nd century, bronze (detail). Art Archive / Musée de la Civilisation Gallo-Romaine Lyons / Dagli Orti

Shepard's Calender, medieval woodcut. Culver Pictures

Janus. Culver Pictures

Aylett Sammes, *Druid*, 1676, from *Britanna Antiqua Illustrata*. British Museum, London. HIP / Scala / Art Resource, N.Y.

Charles Cousen, *The Maypole*, 19th-century engraving after the painting by Joseph Nash. New York Public Library Picture Collection

Leo, 17th-century engraving. Snark / Art Resourse, N.Y.

Pomona, Roman goddess of the harvest, 1st century C.E., Uffizi, Florence. Scala / Art Resource, N.Y.

Aylett Sammes, *The Wicker Image*, 1676, from *Britannia Antiqua Illustrata*. British Museum, London. Art Archive

"Halloween," in *The Delineator*, 1919. New York Public Library Picture Collection

Saturnalia, engraving after drawing by J. R. Weguelin. Culver Pictures

Odin, 1862, woodcut by Ferdinand Schmidt after the drawing by Ludwig Burger. AKG Images

INDEX